CROSSWORDS WORD SEARCHES
LOGIC PUZZLES & SURPRISES!

mind STRETCHERS

MUSTARD EDITION

EDITED BY ALLEN D. BRAGDON

Reader's Digest

The Reader's Digest Association, Inc.
New York / Montreal

Project Staff

PROJECT EDITOR
Robert Ronald

PUZZLE EDITOR
Allen D. Bragdon

PRINCIPAL PUZZLE AUTHORS
Peter De Schepper,
Frank Coussement

CONTRIBUTING PUZZLE AUTHORS
John Samson,
Ron Grosset

SERIES ART DIRECTOR
Andrée Payette

DESIGNER
Craig Brown

PRODUCTION ART
Chris A. Cant

ILLUSTRATIONS
BrainSnack®

COPY EDITOR
Madeline Coleman

PROOFREADER
Penny Grearson

MANAGER, ENGLISH BOOK EDITORIAL
Pamela Johnson

VICE PRESIDENT, BOOK EDITORIAL
Robert Goyette

The Reader's Digest Association, Inc.

PRESIDENT AND CHIEF EXECUTIVE OFFICER
Tom Williams

EXECUTIVE VICE PRESIDENT, RDA & PRESIDENT, NORTH AMERICA
Dan Lagani

EXECUTIVE VICE PRESIDENT, RDA & PRESIDENT, ALLRECIPES.COM
Lisa Sharples

EXECUTIVE VICE PRESIDENT, RDA & PRESIDENT, EUROPE
Dawn Zier

ISBN 978-1-55475-082-5

Address any comments about *Mind Stretchers, Mustard Edition* to:

Reader's Digest Association (Canada) ULC
Book Series Editor
1100 Rene-Levesque Blvd. West
Montreal, Quebec H3B 5H5
Canada

To order copies of this or other editions of the *Mind Stretchers* book series,
call 1-800-846-2100 in the United States and 1-800-465-0780 in Canada.

Visit us on the Web, in the United States at **rd.com**
and in Canada at **readersdigest.ca**

Printed in the United States of America

Contents

Dear Puzzler,

"Use it or lose it!" is more than just a catchy phrase—it has particular significance for those of us battling to keep our wits about us as we age. Research in the cognitive sciences confirms that the stimulation of important centers in the brain not only dramatically slows the natural decline of one's mental powers, but in fact helps improve the function of brain cells. It is also important to understand that the brain's different skills don't compete with each other for space or resources, but rather support one another.

The mental exercises in this volume are designed to challenge a variety of real-world brain skills in entertaining ways: logical deductive reasoning; creative visualization of forms; manipulation of the symbols and rules of mathematical computation; and application of verbal expression and grammatical logic to identify solutions to problems presented in non-verbal ways. A good illustration of how different skills team together can be found in that cluster of techniques and abilities loosely referred to as "creativity."

Brainstorming is a right-brain activity to the extent that it's nonjudgmental, and it's "divergent" rather than "convergent" in the sense that it's not striving toward a single "right" answer. But to really get results, any brainstorming session must be followed by critical evaluation; you have to analyze the logic of each idea to sort the good from the bad. Conversely, pushing a simple idea to its logical conclusion may lead to a counterintuitive conclusion that is sometimes referred to as the "Eureka!" effect.

Number manipulation is a classic left-brain skill, and your left hemisphere will come into play as you work on number puzzles. But many of those puzzles also have visual elements that tap into right-brain skills, such as analyzing a collection of numbers both in terms of its abstract mathematical pattern and its spatial pattern, as laid out on the page. Other puzzles present logical left-brain conundrums in a visual format that may require a contribution from the right brain's spatial-IQ regions.

Different minds work in different ways, and you may find that your approach to solving one of these puzzles is different from that of a friend or partner. For that reason, many of these exercises are fun to do in pairs.

Allen D. Bragdon

Mind Stretchers Puzzle Editor

■ Meet the Authors

Allen D. Bragdon Allen describes himself as "the whimsical old dog with puzzle experience and a curious mind." He is a member of the Society for Neuroscience, founding editor of *Games* magazine and editor of the Playspace daily puzzle column, formerly syndicated internationally by the *New York Times*. The author of dozens of books of professional and academic examinations and how-to instructions in practical skills, Allen is also the director of the Brainwaves Center.

PeterFrank PeterFrank was founded in 2000. It is a partnership between High Performance bvba, owned by Peter De Schepper, and Frank Coussement bvba, owned by Frank Coussement. Together they form a dynamic, full-service content provider specialized in media content.They have more than twenty years of experience in publishing management, art/design and software development for newspapers, consumer magazines, special interest publications and new media.

BrainSnack® The internationally registered trademark BrainSnack® stands for challenging, language-independent, logical puzzles and mind games for kids, young adults and adults. The brand stands for high-quality puzzles. Whether they are made by hand, such as visual puzzles, or generated by a computer, such as sudoku, all puzzles are tested by the target group they were made for before they are made available. In order to guarantee that computer-generated puzzles can actually be solved by humans, BrainSnack® makes programs that only use human logic algorithms.

■ Meet the Puzzles

Mind Stretchers is filled with a delightful mix of classic and new puzzle types. To help you get started, here are instructions, tips and examples for each.

WORD GAMES

Crossword Puzzles

Clues. Clues. Clues.

Clues are the deciding factor that determines crossword solving difficulty. Many solvers mistakenly think strange and unusual words are what makes a puzzle challenging. In reality, crossword constructors generally try to avoid grid esoterica, opting for familiar words and expressions.

For example, here are some actual clues you'll be encountering and their respective difficulty levels:

LEVEL 1   *The Canterbury* ___
LEVEL 2   U2 album *Rattle and* ___
LEVEL 3   U.S. President who spoke Dutch
LEVEL 4   "Musicians in the Orchestra" painter
LEVEL 5   City-shrinking foe of Superman

Clues to amuse. Clues to educate. Clues to challenge your mind.

All the clues are there—what's needed now are your answers.

Happy solving!

Word Searches

by PeterFrank

Both kids and grownups love 'em, making word searches one of the most popular types of puzzle. In a word search, the challenge is to find hidden words within a grid of letters. In the typical puzzle, words can be found in vertical columns, horizontal rows or along diagonals, with the letters of the words running either forward or backward. Usually, you'll be given a list of words to find. But to make word searches harder, puzzle writers sometimes just point you in the right direction—they might tell you to find 25 foods, for example. Other twists include allowing words to take right turns, or leaving letters out of the grid.

Hints: *One of the most reliable and efficient searching methods is to scan each row from top to bottom for the first letter of the word. So if you are looking for "violin" you would look for the letter "v." When you find one, look at all the letters that surround it for the second letter of the word (in this case, "i"). Each time you find a correct two-letter combination (in this case, "vi"), you can then scan either for the correct three-letter combination ("vio") or the whole word.*

Word Sudoku

by PeterFrank

Sudoku puzzles have become hugely popular, and our word sudoku puzzles bring the much-loved challenge to word puzzlers.

The basic sudoku puzzle is a 9 x 9 square grid, split into 9 square regions, each containing 9 cells. You need to complete the grid so that each row, each column and each 3 x 3 frame contains the nine letters from the black box shown above the grid.

There is always a hidden nine-letter word in the diagonal from top left to bottom right.

EXAMPLE

SOLUTION

T	E	W	L	A	B	C	G	R
G	R	L	W	T	C	E	B	A
B	C	A	E	G	R	W	T	L
E	A	B	C	R	L	T	W	G
W	L	C	G	E	T	R	A	B
R	G	T	B	W	A	L	E	C
C	W	E	A	L	G	B	R	T
A	B	R	T	C	E	G	L	W
L	T	G	R	B	W	A	C	E

NUMBER GAMES

Sudoku

by PeterFrank

The original sudoku number format has become amazingly popular the world over due to its simplicity and challenge.

The basic sudoku puzzle is a 9 x 9 square grid, split into 9 square regions, each containing 9 cells. Complete the grid so that each row, each column and each 3 x 3 frame contains every number from 1 to 9.

EXAMPLE

SOLUTION

7	4	2	1	6	5	8	9	3
9	3	5	2	4	8	7	6	1
8	6	1	7	3	9	5	2	4
2	1	3	9	5	4	6	8	7
6	5	9	8	7	3	1	4	2
4	7	8	6	1	2	3	5	9
1	8	6	4	9	7	2	3	5
5	2	4	3	8	1	9	7	6
3	9	7	5	2	6	4	1	8

As well as classic sudoku puzzles, you'll also find sudoku X puzzles, where the main diagonals must also include every number from 1 to 9, and sudoku twins with two overlapping grids.

Kakuro

by PeterFrank

These puzzles are like crosswords with numbers. There are clues across and down, but the clues are numbers. The solution is a sum which adds up to the clue number.

Each number in a black area is the sum of the numbers that you have to fill in to the next empty boxes. The empty boxes that make up the sum are called a run. The sum of the across run is written above the diagonal in the black area, while the sum of the down run is written below the diagonal.

Runs can only contain the numbers 1 through 9, and each number in a run can only be used once. The gray boxes only contain odd numbers and the white only contain even numbers.

EXAMPLE

SOLUTION

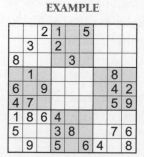

LOGIC PUZZLES

Binairo®

by PeterFrank

Binairo® puzzles look similar to sudoku puzzles. They are just as simple and challenging but that is where the similarity ends.

There are two versions: odd and even. The even puzzles feature a 12 x 12 grid. You need to complete the grid with zeros and ones, until there are 6 zeros and 6 ones in every row and every column. No more than two of the same number can be next to or under each other. Rows or columns with exactly the same combination are not allowed.

EXAMPLE   SOLUTION

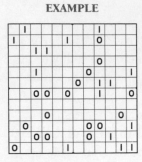

The odd puzzles feature an 11 x 11 grid. You need to complete the grid with zeros and ones until there are 5 zeros and 6 ones in every row and column.

Keep Going

In this puzzle, start on a blank square of your choice and connect as many blank squares as possible with one single continuous line. You can only connect squares along vertical and horizontal lines, not along diagonals. You must continue the connecting line up until the next obstacle—ie, the rim of the box, a black square or a square that has already been used. You can change directions at any obstacle you meet. Each square can only be used once. The number of blank squares left unused is marked in the upper square. There is more than one solution, but we only include one solution in our answer key.

EXAMPLE   SOLUTION

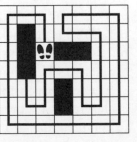

Number Cluster

by PeterFrank

Number Cluster puzzles are language-free, logical numerical problems. They consist of cubes on a 6 x 6 grid. Numbers have been placed in some of the cubes, while the rest are empty. Your challenge is to complete the grid by creating runs of the same number and length as the number supplied. So where a cube with the number 5 has been included on the grid, you need to create a run of five number 5's, including the cube already shown. The run can be horizontal, vertical or both horizontal and vertical.

EXAMPLE   SOLUTION

Pixel Fun

The objective in this puzzle is to reveal a hidden image by coloring in grid squares. You have an 11 x 11 grid with numbers printed outside the grid. The numbers on the outer border, against the black or the white background, indicate the total number of black or white squares on a column or a row. The numbers on the inner border indicate the largest group of adjacent black or white squares to be found anywhere on that column or row. For instance, if there is a 6 on the outer ring and a 2 on the inner ring against a white background, then there are 6 white blocks in that row, and the biggest group or groups consist of a maximum of 2 adjacent white blocks.

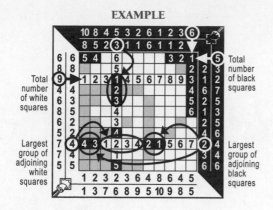

EXAMPLE

Total number of white squares

Total number of black squares

Largest group of adjoining white squares

Largest group of adjoining black squares

Sport Maze

This puzzle is presented on a 6 x 6 grid. Your starting point is indicated by a red cell with a ball and a number. Your objective is to draw the shortest route from the ball to the goal, the only square without a number. You can only move along vertical and horizontal lines, but not along diagonals. The figure on each square indicates the number of squares the ball must be moved in the same direction. You can change directions at each stop.

Cage the Animals

This puzzle presents you with a zoo divided into a 16 x 16 grid. Different animals are included on the grid that need to be separated. Draw lines that will completely divide up the grid into smaller squares, with exactly one animal per square. The squares should not overlap.

EXAMPLE

SOLUTION

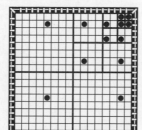

Throughout *Mind Stretchers* you will find unique mazes, visual conundrums and other colorful challenges, each developed by maze master Dave Phillips. Each comes with a new name and unique instructions. Our best advice? Patience and perseverance. Your eyes will need time to unravel the visual secrets.

BrainSnack® Puzzles

To solve a BrainSnack® puzzle, you must think logically. You'll need to use one or several strategies to detect direction, differences and/ or similarities, associations, calculations, order, spatial insight, colors, quantities and distances. A BrainSnack® ensures that all the brain's capacities are fully engaged. These are brain sports at their best!

Weather Charts

We all want to know the weather forecast, and here's your chance to figure it out! Arrows are scattered on a grid. Each arrow points toward a space where a weather symbol should be, but the symbols cannot touch each other vertically, horizontally or diagonally. A symbol cannot be placed on top of an arrow. Determine where the symbols should be placed.

You'll also find more than 100 short brain teasers scattered throughout these pages. These puzzles, found on the bottom of the page, will give you a little light relief from the more intense puzzles while still challenging you.

But wait—there's more!

There are additional brain teasers on top of some pages, organized into two categories:

• **QUICK!**: These tests challenge your ability to instantly calculate numbers or recall well-known facts.

• **DO YOU KNOW...**: These more demanding questions probe the depth of your knowledge of facts and trivia.

For the record, we deliberately left out answers to the Quick! and Do You Know... features. We hope that if you don't know an answer, you'll be intrigued enough to open a book and do some research!

■ Master Class: **Addicted to Learning**

The Brain's Reward for Learning New Skills

The natural state of the human brain is a learning state. In fact, it has built-in mechanisms to reward the learning of new skills. The German word *Funktionslust*, which translates loosely as "joy in doing," describes the feeling any living organism gets from doing something it's built to do—and doing it well. For cats, it may be stalking and catching mice. For bees, it may be honing in on the sights and smells of pollen-filled flowers. For humans, it's learning something new and solving problems.

Why Solving Problems Can Put a Smile on Your Face

The prefrontal cortex, located at the very front of the brain's neuron-saturated surface, handles many functions, including language, planning ahead and emotional responses. Not coincidentally, perhaps, regions of the left prefrontal cortex are activated by tasks that use problem-solving skills. Exercises that particularly involve the left side of the brain include verbal puzzles, such as crosswords and other language games, and number-manipulation puzzles. It appears that activities like these, whether they're part of work or leisure, may stimulate adjacent or overlapping regions of the brain linked to happiness. Of course, the feel-good centers of the brain make no distinction between work and play applications. The activity itself stimulates a sense of well-being. This could explain why crossword puzzle-mavens and workaholics seem to be "addicted" to their respective activities of choice.

Different Tasks for Different Sides of the Brain

Neuroscientists have also discovered that the two sides of the prefrontal cortex may be specialized for different emotions. For decades, neurologists have observed that their patients developed different kinds of emotional disorders depending on which side of their prefrontal cortex was damaged by injury or disease. Damage to the left side was linked to depression, while damage to the right side was linked to manic happiness. Based on these observations, they posited a right-hemisphere specialization for sadness and fear, and a left-hemisphere specialization for happiness and eager enthusiasm. Recent brain imaging studies have confirmed that activity in the left side of the prefrontal cortex correlates with positive emotions. Other research, using modern brain scanning technology, indicates that people with symptoms of depression show less activity in the left side of their prefrontal cortex than other people do.

Dopamine: Helping You to Tackle New Challenges—and Enjoy Doing It

Another link between mental exercise and mood lies in the neurotransmitter chemicals generated by the limbic system, an ancient collection of alerting and action-provoking parts of the brain, located below the more recently-evolved cortex.

When the brain encounters something new, studies of both laboratory animals and humans show increased levels in the amygdala of a neurotransmitter called dopamine. The amygdala is the part of the limbic system that alerts the brain to new data, and dopamine imparts a sense of well-being—which can feel like a reward for whatever triggers its production. It seems to be involved in the early stages of learning, when an environment confronts the brain with a new situation that deserves attention.

Dopamine levels also rise in the prefrontal cortex when the brain applies itself to working memory tasks. These require holding onto data long enough to use it to solve problems, or to evaluate new data for whether it could help you achieve a certain goal.

In a recent study, researchers found that elevated dopamine levels coincided with a person's learning curve. A sharp spike accompanied a rapid, steep curve, while more prolonged dopamine elevation occurred with a longer, slower learning period. High dopamine levels seem to be sustained as long as a task remains new and challenging—that is, as long as you're still learning. Once you've learned a skill

and acted it out so many times that it becomes routine and predictable, your brain no longer provides a reward for performing it. That may be why so many people resort to stimulants such as caffeine to stay motivated when they have to perform familiar, repetitive routines.

Caffeine: a Smart Drug—in Moderation

Caffeine comes in a host of appealing forms, such as coffee, tea or cola. Many professional writers claim that a cup of nice strong coffee not only helps get the flow of ideas going, but also cures writer's block. Countless employers know that a bottomless coffee pot improves the productivity of employees assigned to boring and repetitive tasks.

Research backs up both claims. Several tests measuring word fluency, writing expansiveness and free association show that caffeine does indeed help with creative tasks. Other studies confirm that caffeine improves performance on highly practiced, repetitive tasks that require simple decisions and fast reactions, such as driving a car, sorting mail or typing text into a computer. Small wonder caffeine is claimed to be the most widely used psychoactive drug in the world.

Given all this, it might be reasonable to assume that caffeine's ability to stimulate would apply to learning and memory tasks as well, and in fact many textbooks would agree. Several studies have shown that caffeine can help you absorb new information, perhaps by improving attention and reaction time, as well as mood and motivation.

Part of the reason for caffeine's motivating power is that it interacts with the same dopamine-producing brain systems that give cocaine and amphetamines their pleasurable effect. But while caffeine can make it easier to learn and perform, it can also worsen your performance, depending on what it is you're trying to do.

Separating the Wheat From the Chaff

It has been shown that as tasks become more complex, caffeine won't help performance and might even hurt it because it can interfere with concentration. Also, caffeine can make it harder to pick out the important data while ignoring what's irrelevant. It may interfere with the ability to keep track of information on an ongoing basis and use it to solve complex problems. These are all components of working memory, which is important for both the performance of trickier tasks and learning new problem-solving techniques. As the working memory load gets heavier, the effect of caffeine changes from good to bad.

In one experiment, for example, some subjects were given caffeine and others were not. They were all told to memorize a set of two to four letters and press a button every time they saw those letters flashed on a screen. EEG brain monitoring showed a distinct activation pattern every time any of the subjects saw the memorized letters. The subjects who had ingested caffeine, however, showed the same brain activation pattern when other letters were flashed. In other words, their brain found it harder to ignore the irrelevant, distracting stimuli and focus just on the relevant data.

Wide Awake, but not Paying Attention

Other studies have confirmed that caffeine may impede voluntary attention, a deliberate focus on certain data, while raising involuntary attention, or distraction by irrelevant stimuli. This can be especially harmful if you're unfamiliar with the task at hand, although caffeine can be helpful in the beginning by speeding reaction time. If the task is fairly simple and doesn't increase in complexity, the more times the task is repeated and practiced, the more caffeine will help performance. In effect, it helps to keep you from getting bored. But if the task becomes more complex, the quicker caffeine-induced reaction time is offset by a loss of focus and distraction, and your initially improved performance will get worse.

Here's another example of caffeine's varying effects on the performance of simple and complex tasks. Caffeine can improve performance on a "digits forward" test, where the tester reads a series of numbers out loud (say, 3, 8, 7, 9, 5) and the testee must repeat them back. However, on a "digits backward" test, in which the respondent must repeat the numbers in reverse order—a task that places a heavier burden on working memory—caffeine tends to make performance worse.

For a real-world example, consider another study performed on office managers in a workplace setting. When the managers were given quantities of coffee 400 mg in excess of their usual daily consumption (the equivalent of about four extra cups of coffee), their reaction time improved, which helped them perform better on simple tasks that required simple, rapid responses. But as the tasks became more complex, the managers showed poorer utilization of opportunity—a much more important predictor of managerial success—and their performance declined. "Utilization of opportunity" means using information on an ongoing basis to inform decisions, and requires monitoring and organizing actions that happen one after another. For this important type of executive thinking, simple response speed is less important, and may in fact harm performance by resulting in poorly thought-out decisions.

The Link Between Addictive Substances and the Brain's Natural Reward System

It is possible that a brain denied the stimulation it needs to activate its own reward systems may look for rewards in other ways. On one level, that may be what's happening when intellectual or emotional deprivation leads to drug and alcohol abuse.

Some experimental evidence shows that success in solving mental puzzles boosts not only dopamine levels but also those of the hormone testosterone—an effect which can feel good. However, while elevated testosterone levels do not necessarily lead to violent behavior, violent behavior does raise testosterone. It is tempting to speculate that when people—especially boys and young men—become violent, they may be seeking the kind of testosterone rush that an intellectually unfulfilling environment denies them.

The kinds of reward systems that reinforce survival-related behavior, whether violent or peaceful, always involve brain-chemical molecules. One of the reasons people become addicted to drugs is that those drugs contain molecules that mimic the structure of molecules in the brain's own reward system. Nicotine, cocaine, alcohol and heroin all raise dopamine levels. But so does engaging in literal and metaphorical puzzles which require your brain to handle new data and propose novel solutions—and puzzles are a lot better for you!

Solving problems and learning new things let you feel good while doing something good for your brain. It's perfectly legal, and, at least for now, tax-free.

—Allen D. Bragdon

★ Optical Illusions

All the words are hidden vertically, horizontally or diagonally, both forward and backward. The letters that remain unused form a sentence from left to right.

```
L S N O I T C U R T S N O C X
T E P A T T E R N W D P O E T
A D O S E S N E L I O O T P T
D E T N E N R P O N R R E E U
R C T R A E C R Z T O R C E N
A E N U H R O O O C S E T T N
O I G C L H D P N P O T F H E
B V S N C A S O E E A I I G L
S E F T A D L C D P S N G I E
S A H G N H T U E A E A U L F
E C E I E I C R C P V O R I F
H P L N V S T U L A A I E W E
C B T E R U T P I G M E N T C
I O A N R O V A R I A N T C T
I I S E N A C O L O O K T A I
R C O N V I N C E T B L E T O
I S E E N O N E M O N E H P D
S E P T H A F T E R I M A G E
```

AFTERIMAGE
APERTURE
BLIND SPOT
CHANGE
CHESSBOARD
CHOROID
CONES
CONSTRUCTIONS
CONVINCE
CORNEA
CORTEX
DECEIVE
ESCHER
FIGURE
FOVEA
GESTALT
IRIS
LENSES
LEONARDO DA VINCI
LOOK
MACULA LUTEA
PATTERN
PERSPECTIVE
PHENOMENON
PIGMENT
PONZO
RETINA
RODS
SCLERA
TUNNEL EFFECT
TWILIGHT
VARIANT

TRANSADDITION

Add one letter to SPANNER ART and rearrange the rest, to see things more clearly.

★ Binairo®

Complete the grid with zeros and ones until there are 6 zeros and 6 ones in every row and every column. No more than two of the same number can be next to or under each other. Rows or columns with exactly the same content are not allowed. There is only one valid solution.

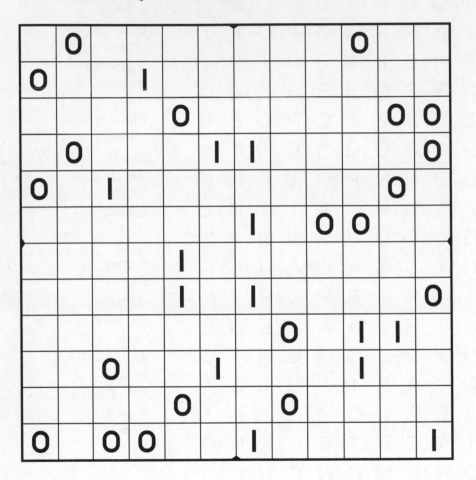

CHANGELINGS

Each of the three lines of letters below should spell the name of a well-known English poet. The lines have, however, been mixed up. Four letters from the first name are now in the third line, four letters from the third name are in the second and four letters from the second name are in the first. The remaining letters are in their original places. What are the poets' names?

LRNGHEOLOS

WOFDEWARTZ

WITLGORFLD

★ Familiar Address by Karen Peterson

28 Edge along
29 Make amends
30 Pilot's "OK"
31 Vera Wang design
33 See 22 Down
36 Kind of phone
37 Elaborated
39 *Mary Poppins* chimney sweep
40 *For Your Eyes Only* director John
42 Bridge alternative
43 *Charmed* actress Milano
45 Copyediting mark
46 Kunis in *Black Swan*
47 Babe Ruth's 2,211
48 Made a putt
49 Dog food brand
50 *American Gigolo* actor
51 Can't stand
52 "How do you like ___ apples?"

ACROSS
1 Liszt's teacher
5 Blade site
10 South Beach ___
14 Curtain color
15 *The Canterbury* ___
16 Suffix for major
17 "And now, the ___ of the story"
18 Cancel a mission
19 Bash
20 Bob Dylan classic
23 Hyacinth, for one
24 ___ *the Mood for Love*
25 "Chili today, hot ___"
28 Traditional
32 French story
33 Flora and fauna
34 Craggy crest
35 *Peter Pan* dog
36 Close-knit group

37 Venetian VIP, once
38 Gold of *Entourage*
39 "Button" site
40 Twins share them
41 First Lady of 2011
43 Adjusts, as a suit
44 ___ Stanley Gardner
45 Lawrence Durrell novel
46 Billy Crystal film
53 Beam in a bridge
54 Prevaricators
55 Remini on *The King of Queens*
56 Fuzzy stuff
57 Source of the Orinoco
58 "A Dream" artist
59 Plays quizmaster
60 ___ *Revolution* (Bob Marley album)
61 Adjudge

DOWN
1 Hairy wave
2 Pacer in *Cars 2*
3 Whilom
4 Yellow turnip
5 Track building
6 "Shish" dish
7 1990s Expo manager
8 Area
9 Approximation
10 Answer the critics of
11 *Star* topic
12 "At Last" singer James
13 Driver's ed student
21 Stubborn critter
22 Natalie's *Black Swan* role
25 Brunchtime, perhaps
26 Donkey Kong" company
27 Frenzied

★ Madonna

All the words are hidden vertically, horizontally or diagonally, both forward and backward. The letters that remain unused form a sentence from left to right.

```
M A D O N N A H A S B E E P N
O N E O S N O I S S E F N O C
F T S H E E Y E N T I R B P O
B Y I S G N G Y E S H T P M N
H E L N E O A O A M C E R U T
N O D A N C E R N D T S E S R
O R F N T C C H E R I S H I O
P O E R K I P U U M R L T C V
F P E I S C L O S C A R O A E
A S W U T R I E F I C F M H R
S W M E N L D R C R O C C O S
H E O S A R U R E W O P T E I
I R D N U L E A E V C Z U L A
O T E O U M T N G G A R E E L
N F L O M I R H O M N M O N R
E U G O V E T H Y C A I N T H
I R C E D A R A P T I H S T Y
Y E M U S I C V I D E O A R S
```

FROZEN
GAULTIER
HIT PARADE
HOLIDAY
ICON
IDOL
ITALY
LOURDES
MAVERICK
MEN
MODEL
MOTHER
MUSIC
MUSIC VIDEO
OSCAR
PENN
POP MUSIC
POWER
RITCHIE
ROCCO
SINGER
SUCCESS
VOGUE
WEALTHY

ACTRESS
BRITNEY
CHERISH
CICCONE

COMMERCIAL
CONFESSIONS
CONTROVERSIAL
CREATIVE

DANCER
EVITA
FAME
FASHION

UNCANNY TURN

Rearrange the letters of these two words to form a cognate anagram, one which is related or connected in meaning to the original phrase. The answer can be one or more words.
THE EARTHQUAKES

★ Cage the Animals

Draw lines that will completely divide up the grid into smaller squares with exactly one animal per square. The squares should not overlap.

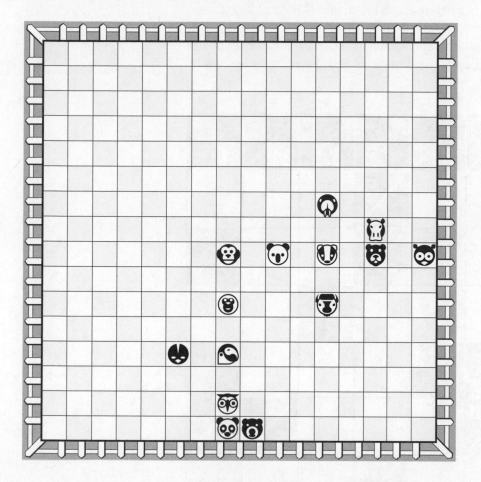

DOUBLE JUMBLES

Each line of mixed letters makes the objects described when the letters are rearranged.
GAMEROPETORANEAGN—Two fruits.
RAZOMSHALIDIC—An animal and a reptile.
RAPTORORTUT—A flower and a fish.
VINTOONIOLE—A color and a vegetable.

★ Kakuro

Each number in a black area is the sum of the numbers that you have to fill in to the next empty boxes. The empty boxes that make up the sum are called a run. The sum of the across run is written above the diagonal in the black area and the sum of the down run is written below the diagonal. Runs can only contain the numbers 1 through 9 and each number in a run can only be used once. The gray boxes only contain odd numbers and the white only contain even numbers.

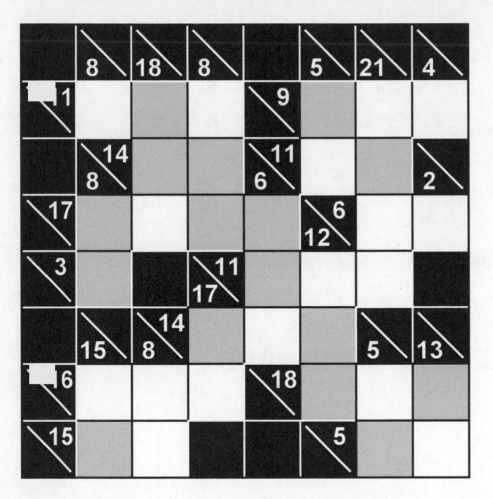

CORE PROBLEM

Three street traders had market stalls side by side each selling the same kind of apples. The first had 33 apples, the second had 29 and the third had 27. Each of them gave the same number of apples for a dollar, yet when they had all sold out they found out that they each had received an equal amount of money! How did it happen?

★ Cheese Escape

What is the minimum number of cheese cubes that the mouse has to eat to escape from the maze?

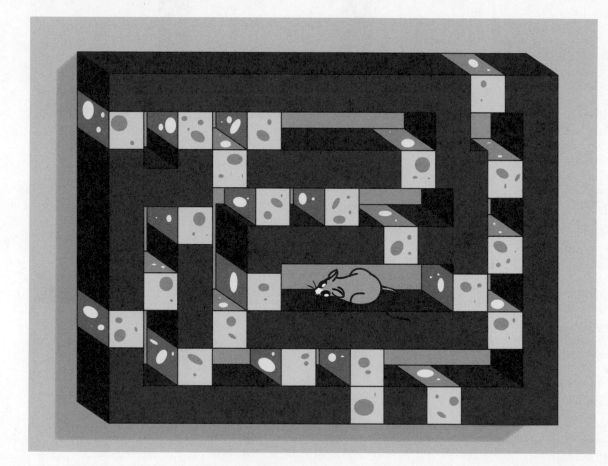

LETTER BLOCKS

Move the letter blocks around so that words are formed on the top and bottom that you can associate with occupations.

★ Director's Chair by Michele Sayer

ACROSS

1 "Open" sign, often
5 Bath accessory
10 Carpet line
14 "... and to ___ good night"
15 Capital ENE of Jerusalem
16 Killer whale
17 *I Kid You Not!* author
18 "Shall we ___?"
19 Whiting and haddock
20 *The Birds* director
23 Cuban film director
24 *Garfield* canine
25 Hostage holder
28 Draw out
32 "___ a Grecian Urn"
33 Befits
34 *Ben-___* (1959)
35 Fibber
36 Binge
37 Aching
38 Comparative suffix
39 Equals
40 "F" on a quiz
41 Ethnology studies
43 Like many tours
44 Served fast and past
45 *Aqualung* group Jethro ___
46 *Schindler's List* director
53 Creep like lava
54 Molecule members
55 Norse war god
56 Vice president in 1804
57 Greyhound station
58 Disney Broadway musical
59 Eminem hit
60 Burnett and Gray
61 Dry run

DOWN

1 *Falcon Crest* valley
2 Tel Aviv carrier
3 One of Snoopy's brothers
4 Mary Alice Young, for one
5 Means of ascent
6 1935 Kentucky Derby winner
7 1980s Dodge model
8 Plants
9 Amusing story
10 David Beckham's sport
11 Suffix for switch
12 *Back in Black* group
13 The Green Hornet's wear
21 PayPal founder Musk
22 Sellouts
25 Baby discomfort
26 "Arrivederci!"
27 30th anniversary gift
28 Acts contentedly
29 "Get ___ of yourself!"
30 Blaspheme
31 Out on a limb
33 Whiz kid?
36 Suitor's song
37 Sloop, for one
39 Dark purple
40 At capacity
42 Alehouse
43 Partygoers
45 *The Lion King* meerkat
46 Has a bawl
47 Tip-sheet seller
48 *The Snowy Day* author ___ Jack Keats
49 1969 Alan Arkin film
50 *Desperate Housewives* divorcée
51 Purges
52 Airborne pest

★ Detectives

All the words are hidden vertically, horizontally or diagonally, both forward and backward. The letters that remain unused form a sentence from left to right.

```
E S C A P E A B U T H O R S O
V U F S U S P P U R S U I T T
I S E M U N G A M R N S E F O
D P U M A N S L A U G H T E R
E E B L S S E C O R P L C R I
N C U E A L Y I M E R S A T O
C T L U V A E M U R D E R R P
E O L U W I R U I E E S S E Y
X T E A E P T E T H I E F T R
E I T S I R H C A H T A G A L
S E S U I C I D E V I T O M A
G M O T L D A L I T M P N Y N
U O R M D E D N K I E U O I I
R R F A D N O S N L E D S A M
D S D R I P T O U H A L I B I
R E Y W A L R E J I R O R A R
U D S E C U L P R I T H P I C
E N W H A N D C U F F S C E S
```

CULPRIT
DEAD
DETECTIVE
DRUGS
ESCAPE
EVIDENCE
FRAUD
FROST
GETAWAY CAR
HANDCUFFS
HOLDUP
JUNKIE
LAWYER
MAGNUM
MANSLAUGHTER
MINOR
MORSE
MOTIVE
MURDER
POIROT
PRISON
PROCESS
PURSUIT
SLEUTH
SUICIDE
SUSPECT
SWINDLE
THIEF
WEAPON

ADDICTED
AGATHA CHRISTIE
ALIBI

ARREST
ASSAULT
BULLET

BURGLARY
CLUE
CRIMINAL

THE 24 PUZZLE

The figure 24 can be expressed in two ways by using the same figure three times—neither of which is 8. If you can discover one of these ways, it should put you on the track of the other.

★ Classic Sudoku

Fill in the grid so that each row, each column and each 3 x 3 frame contains every number from 1 to 9.

		2	1		5			
	3		2					
8				3				
	1						8	
6		9					4	2
4	7						5	9
1	8	6	4					
5			3	8			7	6
	9		5		6	4		8

LETTER BLOCKS

Move the letter blocks around so that words are formed on the top and bottom that you can associate with extremes.

M M A N I U M
M M I X I U M

★ Cage the Animals

Draw lines that will completely divide up the grid into smaller squares with exactly one animal per square. The squares should not overlap.

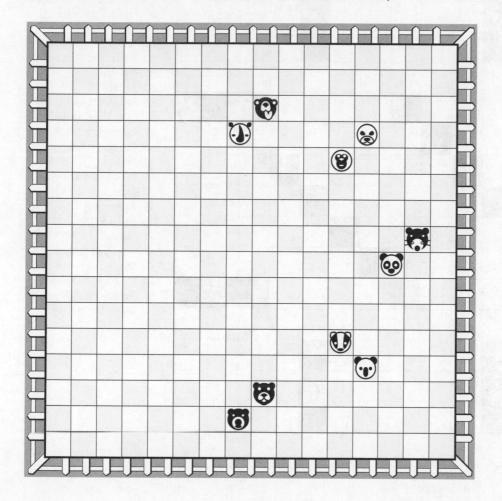

DELETE ONE

Delete one letter from the word BEATERS and rearrange the rest, to get your money back.

★ Themeless by Don Law

22 Mountain passes
25 Aura, slangily
26 "Ice Maiden" of tennis
27 "Help!" star
28 Loafs
29 "Pride ___ before..."
30 WWII hero Murphy
31 Majestic
33 Apparatus
36 Saddam Hussein, e.g.
37 Tony Romo target
39 Aykroyd and Fogelberg
40 Ending for hoop
42 Neiman ___
43 *Good Times* actress
    Rolle
45 Agave fiber
46 Belch forth
47 "Adieu"
48 A bit pretentious
49 Crossed over
50 "Charlie Hustle" Rose
51 Sicilian summer resort
52 Texas flag feature

ACROSS

1 *Black Stallion* boy
5 "Amen!"
10 Judi Dench's title
14 One way to fly
15 Fudd in "Wabbit
    Twouble"
16 "Clue" weapon
17 Strategy
18 "Cut it out!"
19 Viva voce
20 Alcatraz locale
23 Captive of Hercules
24 Corvette roof
25 Springlike
28 Goof off
32 Like Colgate's campus
33 Perth pals
34 Royal possessive
35 City in central Oregon
36 Astounds

37 "Fancy" singer
    McEntire
38 0.0000001 joule
39 Chopped finely
40 Arrive gradually, as
    darkness
41 Bears
43 Deeply embedded
44 "Nay!" sayer
45 "10-4!"
46 Old Glory
53 Paris playground
54 Choppers
55 Air out
56 "And you," to Caesar
57 Benedict XVI's cape
58 Sicilian volcano
59 ___ and Means
    Committee
60 Winona in *Girl,
    Interrupted*

61 Bring up baby

DOWN

1 *Raiders of the Lost Ark*
   reptiles
2 *Shark Tale* dragon fish
3 Ardor
4 In jail
5 Recollect
6 *Ladybugs* actress Graff
7 Detroit financing co.
8 Vacillated
9 Bridge supports
10 Sagging
11 One of two choices
12 Movie-ratings org.:
    Abbr.
13 Congerlike
21 "Ease On Down the
    ___"

★ Dance

All the words are hidden vertically, horizontally or diagonally, both forward and backward. The letters that remain unused form a sentence from left to right.

```
M R T N O I T I T E P M O C R
R A E S A M B A X H U A H Z U
P G M Y T H N P Y S P C Z M M
A G P B P G R S I T R A J É B
R A T I O E I C A C J R R B A
T O A D S Q T Y A L M E O T P
N W T S U W V S E L S N L O Y
E J I E E E I M K E Y A H R E
R O O S C O C N C C M P N T T
N S N Y T N H N G B I C S X A
O A H N B E A S A H T U O O G
C R C D O D N D G D G E Q F I
N N E N K D A I Y N G V I D U
E Z T L A W A L I L I O L Y O
M A O S O C A D S P L C L O C
A F R T O B D R J I V E N C S
L A S A S E O T E L L A B A I
F C I A W L A C T I V I T Y D
```

FOLK DANCE
FOXTROT
GO OUT
HIP-HOP
JAZZ
JIVE
JOY
LAMBADA
MACARENA
MAMBO
MUSIC
PARTNER
PARTY
PHYSIQUE
QUICKSTEP
RAGGA
RUMBA
SALSA
SAMBA
SWING
TANGO
TECHNO
TEMPTATION
TWIST
WALTZ
WEDDING

BALLET
BÉJART
BELLY DANCE
BOLERO

CALYPSO
CANCAN
CLOG DANCE
COMPETITION

DANCING SHOES
DISCO
EXPRESSION
FLAMENCO

CHANGE ONE

Change one letter in each of these two words, to form a common two-word phrase.
SPARE RAVING

★ Cage the Animals

Draw lines that will completely divide up the grid into smaller squares with exactly one animal per square. The squares should not overlap.

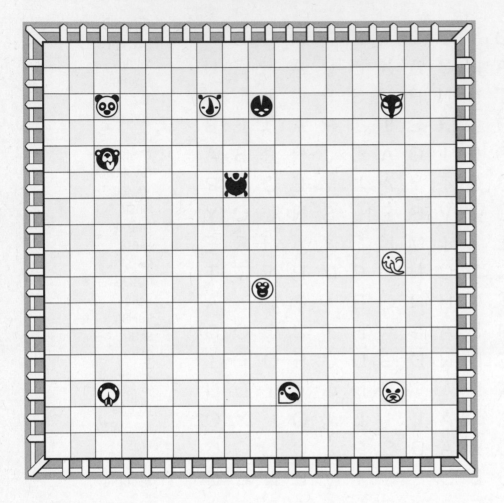

ODD CAP OUT

Which baseball cap (1–6) does not belong?

★ Sudoku Twin

Fill in the grid so that each row, each column and each 3 x 3 frame contains every number from 1 to 9. A sudoku twin is two connected 9 x 9 sudokus.

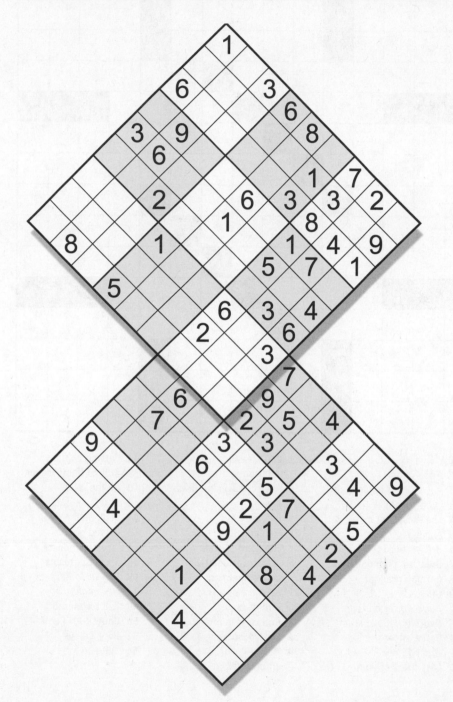

★ This and That by Don Law

ACROSS

1 Recipe directive
5 Goose eggs
10 Morse clicks
14 Big fuss
15 A day's march, for troops
16 Amo, ___, amat
17 Apple of Discord thrower
18 Ryan of the Rangers
19 Mr. Gingrich
20 Waiting-room reading
22 Deems
24 Washington team, for short
25 Algonquian Indian
26 Become pale
29 Bald
33 God of the Koran
34 Think about
35 Room in a casa
36 "___ Amore"
37 *A Death In the Family* author
38 Behind with payments
40 *Damn Yankees* composer
41 Overcomes
42 500 cars
43 Golden Rule word
44 Miss
45 Williams of *Poltergeist*
48 Hoodwinked
52 Collier's entrance
53 From the Old Sod
55 Cab passenger
56 *Dumb & Dumber* type
57 Nick in *Hotel Rwanda*
58 "O.K.!"
59 *House of Dracula* director Kenton
60 *Buffy the Vampire Slayer* role
61 "Country Slaughter"

DOWN

1 Arise (from)
2 ___ Bora, Afghanistan
3 "Cool, man!"
4 *The Aviator* star
5 Acme
6 British jackets
7 Breathing abnormality
8 German grandpa
9 Guards
10 *Harry Potter and the Deathly Hallows* star
11 Grace ender
12 Bird of prey
13 Fast fliers of yore
21 2007 Masters winner Johnson
23 Alpert of Tijuana Brass fame
25 Dessert trays
26 Fundamental
27 Caballero's locale
28 "Sarah Jackman" singer Sherman
29 Attends, as a recital
30 Bird of prey
31 Animal in a roundup
32 Clairvoyants
34 "Cuchi-cuchi" entertainer
36 Cutting canines
39 Bullied baby, maybe
40 Alpine river
42 Assets aplenty
44 Legionnaire Beau
45 Carved gem
46 "Ewww" inducer
47 *Show Boat* tune
48 Boy in *To Kill a Mockingbird*
49 Full of oneself
50 Cubesmith Rubik
51 Poor grades
54 "Vive le ___!"

★ Binairo®

Complete the grid with zeros and ones until there are 6 zeros and 6 ones in
every row and every column. No more than two of the same number can be next
to or under each other. Rows or columns with exactly the same content are not
allowed. There is only one valid solution.

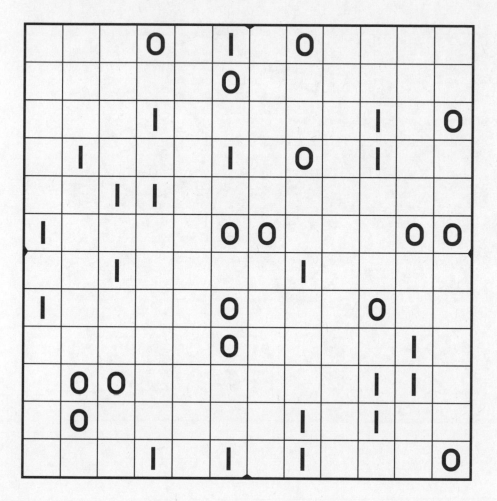

FRIENDS?

What do the following words have in common?
ABLE   EVEN   FAST   THROUGH   DOWN   AWAY   WATER   NECK

★ A Good Impression

Which stamp (A–E) does not originate from any of the rubber stamps above (1–5)?

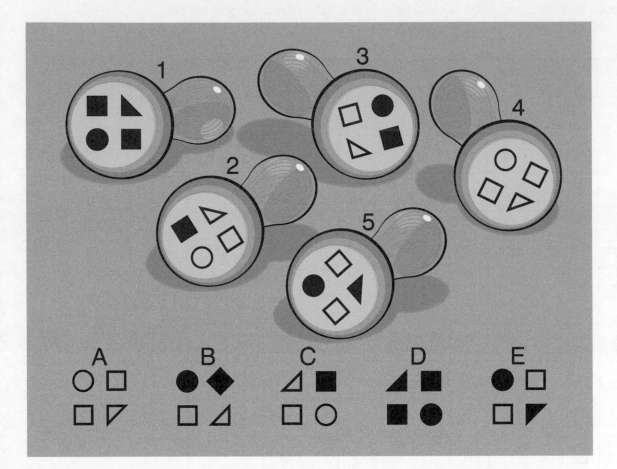

FIRST THINGS FIRST

Identify the well-known proverb from the first letters in each of its words.

L. S. D. L.

★ Weather Forecast

All the words are hidden vertically, horizontally or diagonally, both forward and backward. The letters that remain unused form a sentence from left to right.

```
S P R I N G T I M E A W H H E
A P T H N E P R S N O S A E S
F O A I S W A R M I N G I A R
E P R T H U N D E R B O L T C
A P O S C O L D A S T I S W S
S R M L E H Y U R U S M T A A
M E R D L N O E M O T U O V C
Y C O B N E A F A U U U R E O
G I T U S E N C F I C G M E M
O P S Q U A L L I O S D H N P
L I R E T N I W R R G O O T U
O T E M P E R A T U R E B S T
R A D S N M D R E M M U S A E
O T N O I I O M A D E L H C R
E I U C O R A L W I C U L E A
T O H T I L N O O N N S A R N
E N T D E M F U N P I R I O C
M A R E C O R D S L D A T F A
```

PRECIPITATION
PRESSURE
RADIO
RAIN
RECORDS
SEASONS
SNOW
SPRING
SPRINGTIME
SQUALL
STORM
SUMMER
SUNNY
SUNRISE
TEMPERATURE
THUNDERBOLT
THUNDERSTORM
WARM
WARMING
WINTER

AUTUMN
COLD
COMPUTER
CUMULUS
DROUGHT
FLOOD
FORECAST
HAILSTORM
HEAT WAVE
HOT
HURRICANE
ISOBAR
METEOROLOGY
PATCH OF FOG
POLLEN

DOUBLETALK

What four-letter word can either mean your head or a verb meaning to take care?

★ Shady Puzzler

Which color (1–8) should replace the question mark?

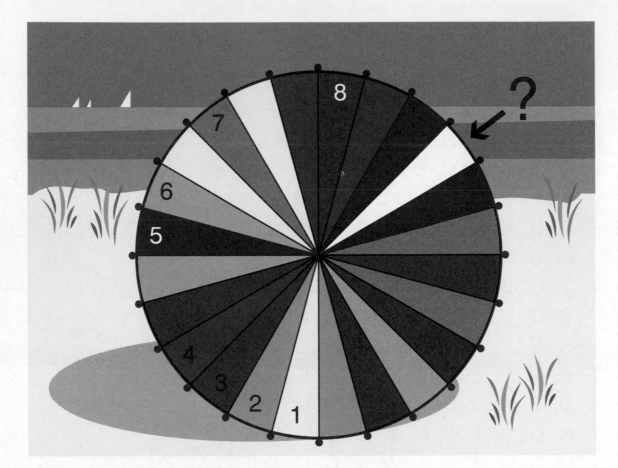

SPOT THE DIFFERENCES

★ Legends of the Game by Michele Sayer

ACROSS

1 Affaire d'honneur
5 Bluenoses
10 *For Your Eyes Only* hero
14 Hence
15 Adams of *CSI: Crime Scene Investigation*
16 Jai ___
17 "Cunning hunter" in Genesis
18 Not so hot
19 Sleeveless garment
20 2004 Wimbledon winner
23 Roadside sign
24 *Heaven ___ Wait* (1978)
25 *Erin Brockovich* director Soderbergh
28 Awful
30 Foolish month: Abbr.
33 *Spartacus* costume
34 10 million equal a joule
35 On the briny
36 Swedish golf legend
39 Hawaii's "Valley Isle"
40 Level, in London
41 Windy City hub
42 Letter before omega
43 *Saturday Night Live* segment
44 Opposed
45 "Billy, Don't ___ Hero"
46 *My Name Is Asher ___:* Potok
47 2010 Wimbledon winner
55 Alan in *The Aviator*
56 County in Ireland
57 *Return of the Jedi* princess
58 *Daily Planet* reporter
59 All lit up
60 Tennyson's title
61 Simians
62 Add golds to a mine
63 "Storms in Africa" singer

DOWN

1 Adjudge
2 Polaris bear
3 Food thickener
4 "The Lion" king of France
5 House of correction
6 "If I Were a ___ Man"
7 Olympic medalist Kulik
8 Will in *The Waltons*
9 "Salt City" of New York
10 Side with eggs
11 Grieg's "___ Trygvason"
12 Valley near San Francisco
13 Fade out
21 Smart-___
22 Crony
25 2011 Tito Puente commemorative
26 Albacore and blue fin
27 Blah feeling
28 "Mending Wall" poet
29 "Fee fi fo fum" sayer
30 ___ *Is Born* (1976)
31 Seckel and Anjou
32 *Findelkind* author
34 *Caprica* actor Morales
35 Biltmore Estate city
37 "Land of Opportunity"
38 Inventive
43 Notice
44 Lets
45 Pentagon VIPs
47 Feed the pigs
48 Adams in *The Apartment*
49 Pond scum
50 Volition
51 "___ Rhythm"
52 ___ *Flux* (2005)
53 Boglike
54 *Family* actress Thompson
55 According to

★ School

All the words are hidden vertically, horizontally or diagonally, both forward and backward. The letters that remain unused form a sentence from left to right.

```
P I H S N R E T N I D I N G C
M U I S A N M Y G N C R E L E
P K S S C H Z I U Q O H A M F
H S T A F F R O O M T S A O O
Y R O S I V R E P U S X U L L
S M R E M G A T N P E N O S K
I T Y F Y O E B H L T O R E H
C R R A G A O O A A H E T S O
S O L O C E T R I C I M I U M
E P B H P O O N S E K L C B E
D E E A U S P G S S G P E J W
O R N L Y E N L R N A P A E O
T R A I N I N G E A R L O C R
S P E W D R O C U D P S C T K
C H I R I L D I R E G H N S H
A D A T I N M S E T O E Y F O
L O L L A N G U A G E S R O W
B I O L O G Y M L E S S O N S
```

BACKPACK
BIOLOGY
BOARDING SCHOOL
CHALK
CLASS PHOTO
CLASSROOM
DRAWING
ENGLISH
EXAM
FOUNTAIN PEN
GEOGRAPHY
GYMNASIUM
HISTORY
HOMEWORK
INTERNSHIP
LANGUAGES
LEDGER
MUSIC
ORAL EXAM
PHYSICS
PLAYGROUND
QUIZ
REPORT
SPORTS
STAFF ROOM
SUBJECTS
SUPERVISOR
TEACHER
TEST
TRAINING

ANAGRAM

Unscramble the letters in the phrase CAMEO DESIGNS to form two words with the same or similar meanings.

★ Cage the Animals

Draw lines that will completely divide up the grid into smaller squares with exactly one animal per square. The squares should not overlap.

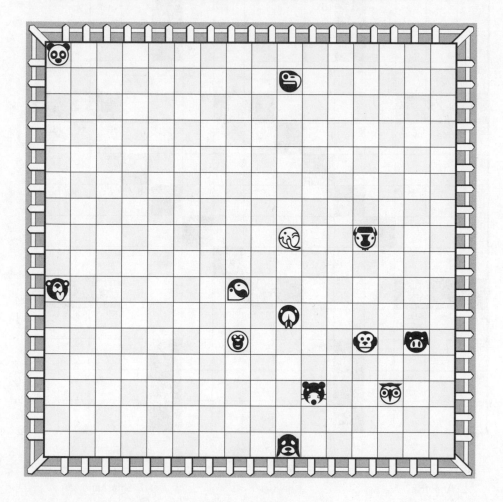

LETTER BLOCKS

Move the letter blocks around so that words are formed on the top and bottom that you can associate with families.

★ Comedy Teams by John McCarthy

ACROSS
1 Knox or Dix
5 Ledger entry
10 Hugh Laurie's alma mater
14 Aunt Bee's charge
15 Age
16 Captive of Hercules
17 Nothing, in Madrid
18 Pyle of Mayberry
19 Healthy look
20 *A Night at the Opera* stars
23 Loom part
24 "Slippery when ___"
25 Washer setting
28 "As Tears Go By" singer Marianne
33 Fugard's *A Lesson From ___*
34 *Common Sense* pamphleteer
35 *Andy Capp* quaff
36 Animal abode
37 Held on
38 *True Colors* actress Merrill
39 Aliens, for short
40 Plainspoken
41 Mideast money
42 Inessential
44 Accelerate
45 Narrow shoe width
46 Carmichael and Fleming
47 *Have Rocket, Will Travel* stars
55 Groovy things
56 Bury
57 Spartan queen of myth
58 Inuit abode
59 *The Hunchback of ___ Dame*
60 Steam hole
61 Nasty
62 Epoxied
63 Historic periods

DOWN
1 Arial, e.g.
2 Moonfish
3 "Ticket to ___": Beatles
4 Trucker
5 Extent
6 Adhesive
7 Fail miserably
8 Bubbly chiller
9 Bullpen activity
10 H's position
11 Lacquered metalware
12 Swan genus
13 Intelligence
21 "When ___ said and done ..."
22 Head of France
25 Ancient Greek physician
26 Carry away, in a way
27 Bing, bang or boom
28 Goat-legged deities
29 "___ We Got Fun?"
30 Barely audible
31 Arm bones
32 Discover
34 "Besides that ..."
37 Bush-hog job
38 Break up
40 "Been there, done that" feeling
41 "Book 'em ___!"
43 Japanese car of yore
44 Odium
46 Alpine river
47 Shipshape
48 Colossal
49 "... ___ tête, Alouette!"
50 Organic compound
51 Famous last words
52 *The Waltons* actor Will
53 Krabappel of *The Simpsons*
54 Admission exams

★ Classic Sudoku

Fill in the grid so that each row, each column and each 3 x 3 frame contains every number from 1 to 9.

	4			1	8	2		
	8		7		5			1
	9	1		2				7
					6			4
		4	9	3	2			8
	6		5	4		7		2
8		2			9			3
							1	6
	1			7				

FIVES AND FOURS

Each line contains a five-letter and four-letter word that have been mixed together (the order of the letters in each word has not been changed). Unmix the two words on each line and write them in the spaces provided. When you're done, find a two-part answer to the clue by reading down the letter columns in the answers.

CLUE: Economic trend?

C D R A E S A M T   _ _ _ _ _   +   _ _ _ _

O L G U I V R U E   _ _ _ _ _   +   _ _ _ _

B W H E I T A R E   _ _ _ _ _   +   _ _ _ _

N B A O K R E N D   _ _ _ _ _   +   _ _ _ _

★ Word Sudoku

Complete the grid so that each row, each column and each 3 x 3 frame contains the nine letters from the black box below. A hidden nine–letter word is in the diagonal from top left to bottom right.

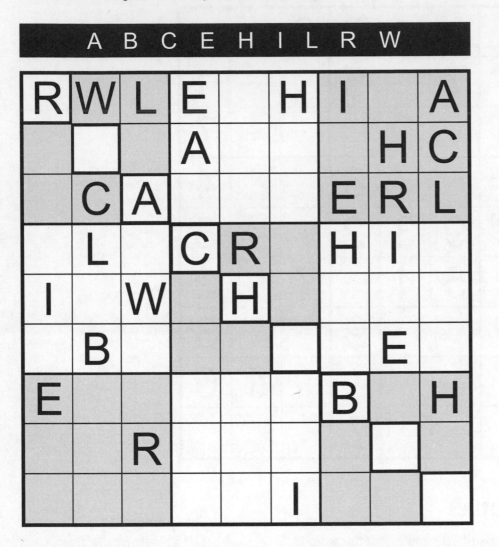

LETTER BLOCKS

Move the letter blocks around so that words are formed on the top and bottom that you can associate with kitchenware.

★ Cubist Problem

Which cube (1–6) cannot be made with the floor plan?

SPOT THE DIFFERENCES

★ Furniture

All the words are hidden vertically, horizontally or diagonally, both forward and backward. The letters that remain unused form a sentence from left to right.

```
T H E W S T E R E O C T C D P
R O R D F R L K U R C H R E N
E L B A T O D I N E A A E T C
T S A U L F N R T I O L H S I
N S T E U M A I R B S C I O T
E A H M X O H O P E R D N F S
P L S O U C O U C H E E G O A
R G B F R D C Y R B W L E O L
A S O A Y T M R O T A I G D P
C Y F T T H E A F N R V A N E
F N O M I E R R L G D E R A R
S T O O L D D B E I F R O T E
N H T S A Y C I H S O Y T S H
W E S P U D O L S E T R S T D
F T T H Q N W O O D S O F A O
U I O E R E N I L C E R R H N
I C O R R R T O F U H B R N I
S H L E E T S A R M C H A I R
```

COMFORT
COUCH
CUPBOARD
DELIVERY
DESIGN
DOOR
FOOD
FOOTSTOOL
GLASS
HANDLE
HATSTAND
HINGE
LIBRARY
LUXURY
PLASTIC
QUALITY
RECLINER
RETRO
SHELF
SIDEBOARD
SINK
SLEEP
SOFA
STEEL
STEREO
STOOL
STORAGE
SYNTHETIC
TABLE
TRENDY
WOOD

ARCHITECT
ARMCHAIR
ATMOSPHERE
BATH
BEDSIDE TABLE
CARPENTER
CHAIR
CHEST
CHEST OF DRAWERS

IS IT RIGHT?

Which of these four words is misspelled?

A) irrideemable

B) irreverent

C) irrevocable

D) irritable

★ Cage the Animals

Draw lines that will completely divide up the grid into smaller squares with exactly one animal per square. The squares should not overlap.

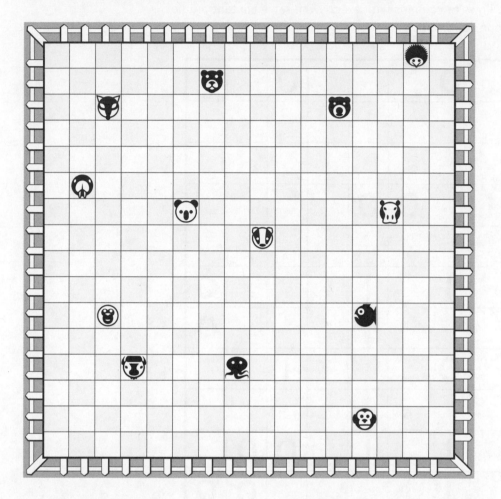

CHANGELINGS

Each of the three lines of letters below should represent the name of a kind of theatrical entertainment. The letters have been mixed up like this: five letters have been taken from the first line and placed in the third, five from the third are in the second, and five from the second are in the first. The remaining four letters in each line are in their original positions.

    L A B T Q S I U E
    O U R A E M R M E
    N E L M D O A P M

Can you sort them out in twenty seconds? Starting ... NOW!

★ Binairo®

Complete the grid with zeros and ones until there are 5 zeros and 6 ones in every row and every column. No more than two of the same number can be next to or under each other. Rows or columns with exactly the same content are not allowed. There is only one valid solution.

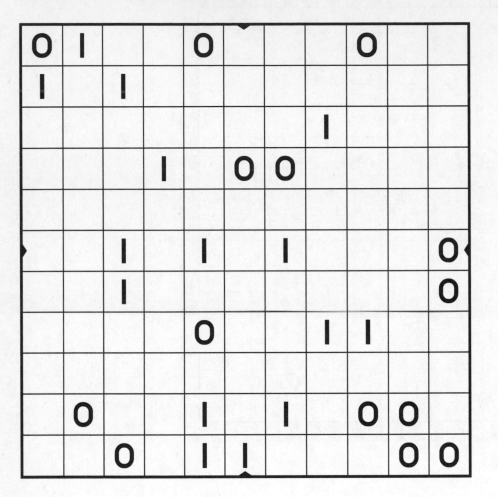

HOW MUCH?

Jones gives Smith as many coins as Smith has. Smith then gives Jones as many coins as Jones has left. They then find that Jones has 36 coins and Smith has 42 coins. How many did each of them have to begin with?

★ Water Conservation

The showerhead on the left uses the most water. Which showerhead (1–6) should you replace it with so that you use a lot less water while showering?

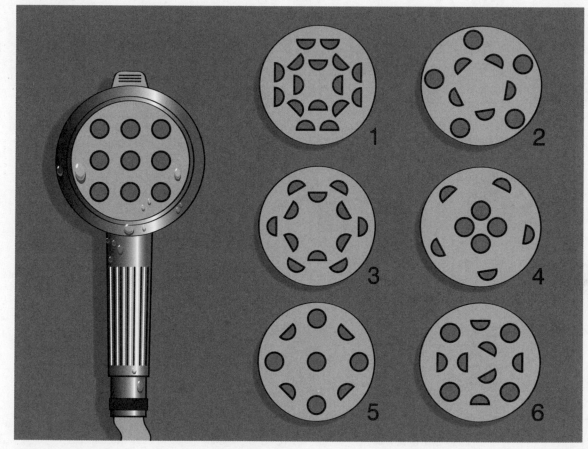

MISSING LETTER PROVERB

Fill in each missing letter, indicated by X, to make a well-known proverb.
XAXXE NXX XANX XOT.

★ Divas by John McCarthy

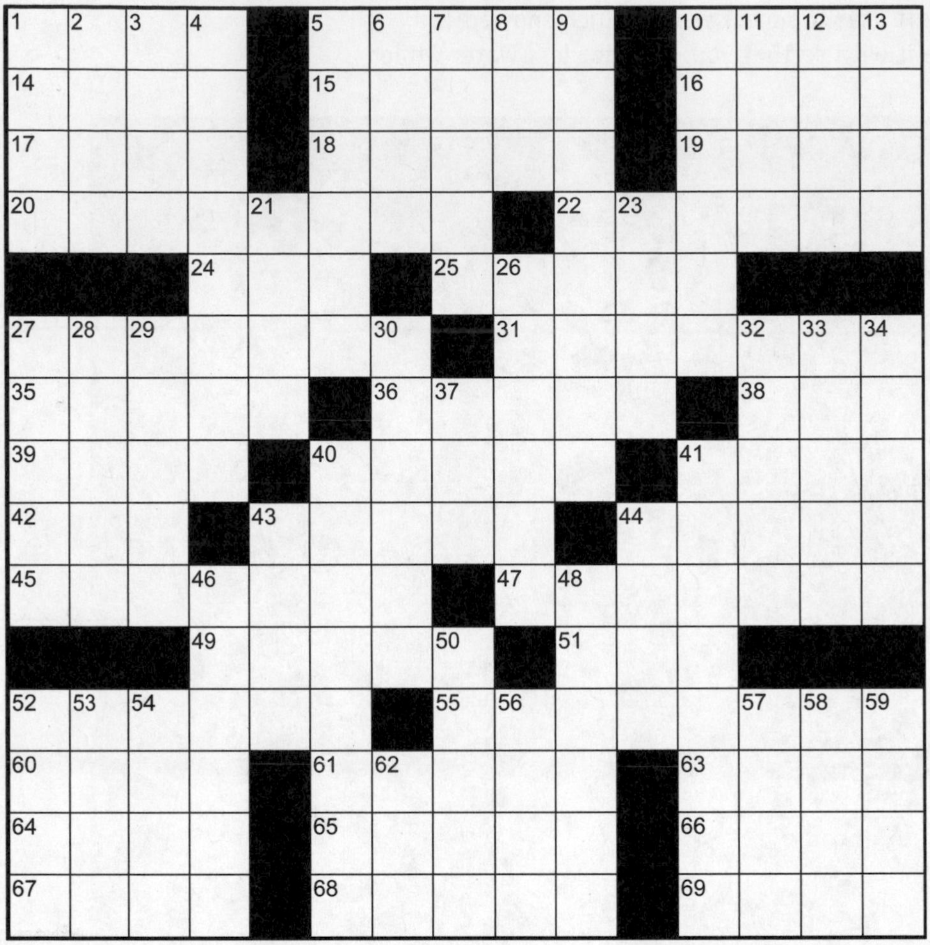

The crossword grid with numbered cells.

ACROSS

1 An egg in Caesar's salad
5 Campground lights
10 Sandler in *The Wedding Singer*
14 Italian tower city
15 "Le Roi d'Yvetot" composer
16 Singer Simone
17 State with assurance
18 Bengal cat
19 "Dinner's ready" sound
20 "Poker Face" singer
22 Circus rings
24 Painter van Eyck
25 Birth-related
27 *Calvin and Hobbes* babysitter
31 "If I Were a Boy" singer
35 Greenhouse gas
36 Missouri tribe
38 Catch the flu
39 Asthmatic sound
40 Caulking material
41 Golden vein
42 Ovine parent
43 Smooth change
44 Japanese noodles
45 "Material Girl" singer
47 "Hips Don't Lie" singer
49 Coffeehouse readers
51 1989 Metallica hit
52 Chicken scratch
55 "Beautiful" singer Christina
60 Baghdad locale
61 Cantina cookware
63 Unit of matter
64 Café card
65 "Pet" annoyance
66 In the altogether
67 NBA great Maravich
68 Chair designer
69 Fizzles out

DOWN

1 "Fire" gem
2 ___ *Las Vegas* (1964)
3 Pre-owned
4 "Family Affair" singer Blige
5 Ceremonial prayer
6 "... nine, ten, ___ fat hen"
7 Fox in *Transformers*
8 Cellist Jacqueline du ___
9 Plan of attack
10 Ali's trainer Dundee
11 "Us" singer Celine
12 *The King and I* heroine
13 Shiny wheels
21 *The Life of David* ___ (2003)
23 "Love, Me" singer Collin
26 Eases up
27 "Air Music" composer
28 Conductor Seiji
29 Did a shoe repair
30 3 Musketeers filling
32 Wynonna Judd's mom
33 Halloween drink
34 *The Mask of Zorro* heroine
37 *The Hangover* dentist
40 Cruz in *Nine*
41 City between Tampa and Orlando
43 Winter fall
44 *Doctor Who* villainess
46 Cloudy
48 Some ranches
50 Witch Sabrina's cat
52 Airhead
53 Montana tribe
54 Go postal
56 Donated
57 Notions case
58 Was a passenger
59 Iowa State U. city
62 Michele of *Glee*

★ Cage the Animals

Draw lines that will completely divide up the grid into smaller squares with exactly one animal per square. The squares should not overlap.

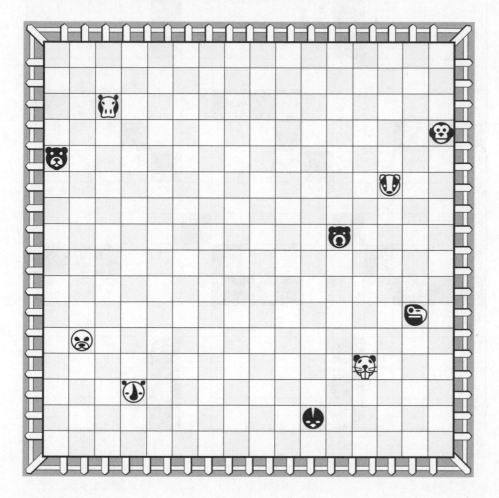

WORDS IN HIDING

Each of the lines below contains the name of a bird, beast or fish. Find them!
Example: "There was a thROB IN his heart."

They both rushed out of the room.
Her tennis is quite good but she lobs terribly.
He was the star linguist of the party.
We clambered up the mountainside, eroded and worn away by the centuries.
Count up to ten, children.
Is there a bench or seat where I can sit down?

★ Gray Scale Extremes by John McCarthy

ACROSS

1 Ally Financial, formerly
5 Basketball
10 ___ Enchanted (2004)
14 Reckless
15 Pond buildup
16 What proofers do
17 Shell competitor
18 Most-quoted Yankee
19 2009 Daniel Day-Lewis film
20 Preakness winner's blanket
23 "Ma'am," in Mexico
24 Derby Day wear
25 ___ Alamos
26 Drop anchor
28 Naughty
31 Gannet
34 Witching ___
35 Menu fish
36 All the president's men
39 Lieutenant
40 "___ It Romantic?"
41 Orderly grouping
42 Negatives
43 90° from north
44 Billiards stick
45 Ply the needle
46 Black Sea port
50 *I Love Lucy* was watched on one
56 Continental coin
57 "___ in Paradise": Poe
58 Early Manitoban
59 "In ___ of flowers ..."
60 Hang like a hummingbird
61 Allege as a fact
62 Studio head
63 Glacial spur
64 Flat fee?

DOWN

1 Snatches
2 *That Girl* girl
3 Happy ___ be
4 Willy Wonka product
5 ___ corpus
6 Composer Speaks
7 "Fee, fi, fo, fum" sayer
8 Western sidekick
9 Where "she sells shells"
10 Blofeld in *Thunderball*
11 *Return of the Jedi* princess
12 *Death in Venice* author
13 Pindar poems
21 Copenhagen coin
22 Old Egypt
26 Horse
27 Banish
28 Piglet's pa
29 "A" in code
30 Overcome gravity
31 Ugly Duckling, actually
32 Columbus locale
33 Can covers
34 *Bonanza* brother
35 Vehicle for Blanche DuBois
37 Minnehaha's mate
38 Riyadh resident
43 "A mouse!"
44 Stick
45 Scrub the tub
47 Start a match
48 "Card Players Quarreling" artist
49 Prevent
50 Judo sash
51 *Los Olvidados* director Buñuel
52 Vicinity
53 Former Jordanian queen
54 Peace symbol
55 NYC PBS station

★ Motorcycle

All the words are hidden vertically, horizontally or diagonally, both forward and backward. The letters that remain unused form a sentence from left to right.

```
N E G A G G A B A K E D B I K
M O T O C R O S S N E S A R E
R I Y R U X U L P O R U D N E
H O R S E P O W E R E V I R D
S O T R U R A C E T R A C K E
P H R A O Z E S D O O R C T L
Y E A N C R U H S N M O H M O
T A V R C I S K T E O R O O O
C D E Y L R D C I A N P P D C
L L L E U E E N S T E G P E R
S I T H T A Y T I D A L E E I
P G T D C O R N O O T C R R A
E H O F H A F E R O N A U F R
E T I O I D E R S A C P R D O
D T N L E T E M L E H S C T I
W D E O N F R A D O A M T H E
A R W I N D B I T R I U M P H
Y A N D P A S S I O N R A I N
```

HEADLIGHT
HELMET
HONDA
HORN
HORSEPOWER
INDICATOR
LEATHER
LUXURY
MIRRORS
MOPED
MOTOCROSS
NORTON
PASSENGER
PASSION
RACE
RACETRACK
SCOOTER
SIDECAR
SPEED
SPEEDWAY
SUZUKI
TRAILER
TRAVEL
TRIUMPH

AIR-COOLED
BAGGAGE
BALANCE
BOXER

CHAIN
CHOPPER
CLUTCH
DRIVER

DUCATI
ENDURO
FREEDOM
HARLEY

UNCANNY TURN

Rearrange the letters of these two words to form a cognate anagram, one which is related or somehow connected in meaning to the original phrase. The answer can be one or more words.

DEBIT CARD

★ Binairo®

Complete the grid with zeros and ones until there are 6 zeros and 6 ones in every row and every column. No more than two of the same number can be next to or under each other. Rows or columns with exactly the same content are not allowed. There is only one valid solution.

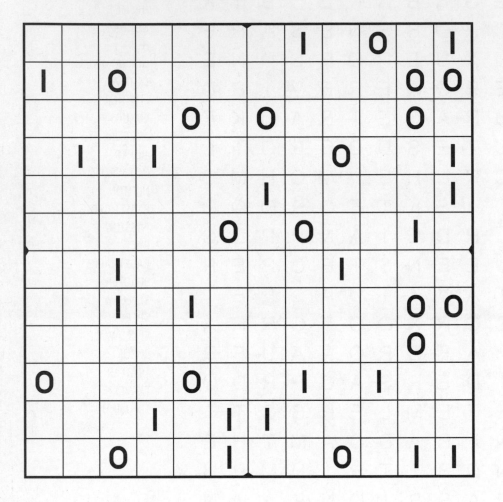

MISH-MATCH

The first word below contains the first three letters of a fruit and the last three letters of a flower, and the second word contains the last three letters of the fruit and the first three letters of the flower.

CAROUS

CONGER

★ Kakuro

Each number in a black area is the sum of the numbers that you have to fill in to the next empty boxes. The empty boxes that make up the sum are called a run. The sum of the across run is written above the diagonal in the black area, and the sum of the down run is written below the diagonal. Runs can only contain the numbers 1 through 9, and each number in a run can only be used once. The gray boxes only contain odd numbers and the white only contain even numbers.

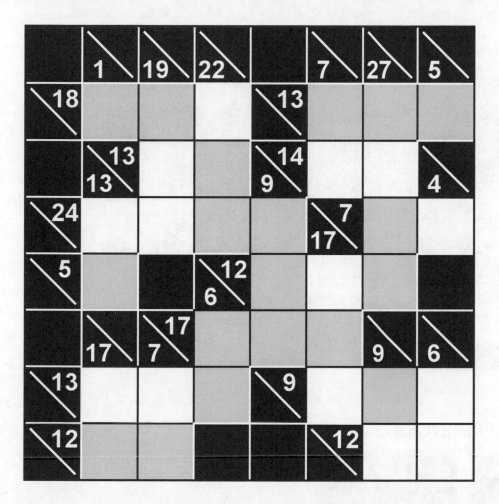

ALL IN A MUDDLE

The first word below contains the first three letters of a bird and the last three letters of an animal, while the second word contains the last three letters of the bird and the first three letters of the animal.

MOLEST

TEAWIT

★ Seeing Red

We see a red tower through an airplane window. With which tower (1–9) on the city plan does this red tower correspond?

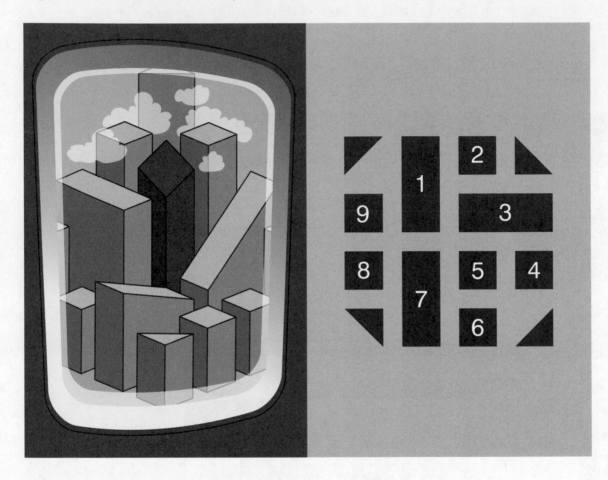

SPOT THE DIFFERENCES

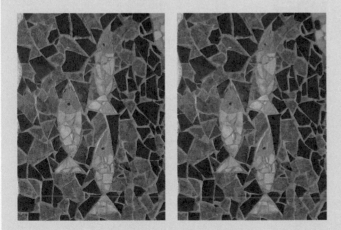

★ Cage the Animals

Draw lines that will completely divide up the grid into smaller squares with exactly one animal per square. The squares should not overlap.

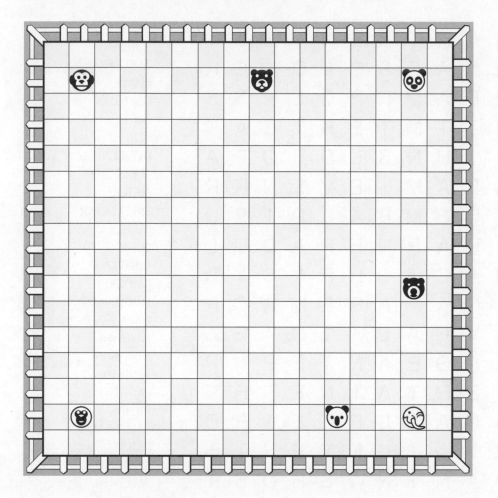

A CORNY QUESTION

A merchant had 21 sacks of grain in store: 7 full, 7 half-full and 7 empty. He wanted to divide them equally among his three sons. How can he do this—without transferring any portion of grain from sack to sack—so that each son will not only have an equal quantity of grain, but also an equal number of sacks?

★ Professions

All the words are hidden vertically, horizontally or diagonally, both forward and backward. The letters that remain unused form a sentence from left to right.

```
M E R C H A N T D E N T I S T
C S T D R N A F S O L D I E R
I F M E E E A M R B C E R S S
T N R T D L T M T E H T E A T
I A E E C I U N S L D R O E A
R I T C H R A M I E V L N R R
C D S T R U E M B A L P I E U
S E I I E U A P N E P A D U L
L M N V H A C T O R R L S Y B
S O I E C N A M A R E M A C R
H C M A A V E A L W T O A E W
T R E S E R G E A N T E P N P
C O E N T E R T A I N E R R E
G L L M A N A G E R E E I R D
S U O I R T A T U K Y E S T I
H A I W P A N T N W S H O S T
E W H D N O F N A T M A K E O
A N A M E C I L O P M E S S R
```

ACTOR
BUILDER
CAMERAMAN
CLOWN
COMEDIAN
CRITIC
DENTIST
DETECTIVE
DOCTOR
EDITOR
ENTERTAINER
FARMER
GUIDE
INNKEEPER
LAWYER
LUMBERMAN
MAID
MANAGER
MERCHANT
MINISTER
PAINTER
PILOT
POLICEMAN
PRIEST
REPORTER
SALESMAN
SERGEANT
SERVANT
SMITH
SOLDIER
TEACHER
WELDER

DELETE ONE

Delete one letter from the word ADMIRERS and rearrange the rest, and get hitched.

★ Classic Sudoku

Fill in the grid so that each row, each column and each 3 x 3 frame contains every number from 1 to 9.

					1		5	
						9		
					3			7
	7		2					6
	1	4		8		2	9	
9	2			5		1	7	3
	8	3	6		5			9
				7	8		4	1
	4							

CHANGE ONE

Change one letter in each of these two words, to form a common two-word phrase.
   Stray in

★ Letter Lining

Which 3 letters should be underlined?

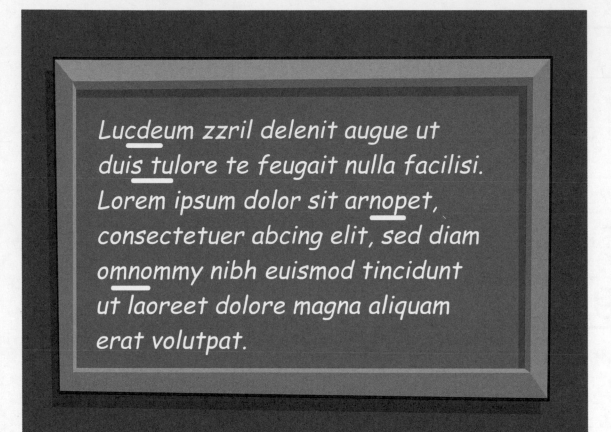

> Lucdeum zzril delenit augue ut
> duis tulore te feugait nulla facilisi.
> Lorem ipsum dolor sit arnopet,
> consectetuer abcing elit, sed diam
> omnommy nibh euismod tincidunt
> ut laoreet dolore magna aliquam
> erat volutpat.

LETTER BLOCKS

Move the letter blocks around so that words are formed on the top and bottom that you can associate with sports.

★ Traffic Light by Karen Peterson

27 Kind of eclipse
28 Adversary
29 Gingery cookie
30 Paddock sound
31 Bubble up
32 Attendant on Artemis
34 Dismounted
37 Oster grooming product
38 The Lower 48, to Hawaiians
40 A Stetson has a broad one
41 "... with a banjo on my ___"
43 Avoided
44 Defend against criticism
46 *Animal House* brother
47 Acts the magpie
48 Shape of "the Big A"
49 Agree
50 Persian Gulf land
51 Approach to the altar
52 Belt
53 New Zealander
54 Puts on the feed bag

ACROSS
1 President #41 or #43
5 Shatter
10 Homophone of Lou
14 "Deal me in" indicator
15 Advantageous
16 "He was," in Caesar's time
17 Brook
18 Nureyev, for one
19 Safeguard
20 Holds for a news flash
23 *On Golden Pond* bird
24 Pigged out
25 Abaft
28 Coffeehouse order
33 "___ Were the Days"
34 *The Nanny Diaries* nanny
35 *Car Talk* network
36 Body art, slangily
37 Spotless
38 Disdainful grimace
39 "Apple cider" gal
40 Goodyear airship
41 Fate
42 Haste
44 "Friendly Skies" flier
45 "Keep a stiff upper ___"
46 Golf tourney
47 "Beat it!"
55 All fired up
56 Love poetry Muse
57 "Ah! Perfido!" is one
58 Sultan of Swat
59 "Alborada del Gracioso" composer
60 Mr. Gingrich
61 *The Call of the Wild* vehicle
62 Dummy Mortimer
63 Place for a speaker

DOWN
1 Jungle-gym features
2 Squad
3 1944 battle site
4 Dependent
5 Frosty's nose
6 Beehive State native
7 Diet ___ Cola
8 "Fresh!" follow-up
9 Aquatic turtle
10 Apartment dweller
11 Cleopatra's maid
12 Roof projection
13 SUVs
21 Piqued
22 Raison d'___
25 Loft
26 "A Whiter ___ of Pale"

★ Cage the Animals

Draw lines that will completely divide up the grid into smaller squares with exactly one animal per square. The squares should not overlap.

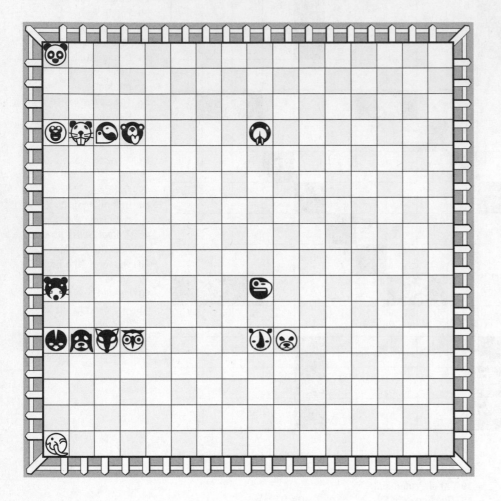

REVERSALS

The first line of each couplet is the definition of a word. The second line is the definition of the same word reversed.
Done by tops.
To drink in drops.

A taste high.
Flew in my eye.

An act good or bad.
Do a good one, my boy.

★ Sudoku Twin

Fill in the grid so that each row, each column and each 3 x 3 frame contains every number from 1 to 9. A sudoku twin is two connected 9 x 9 sudokus.

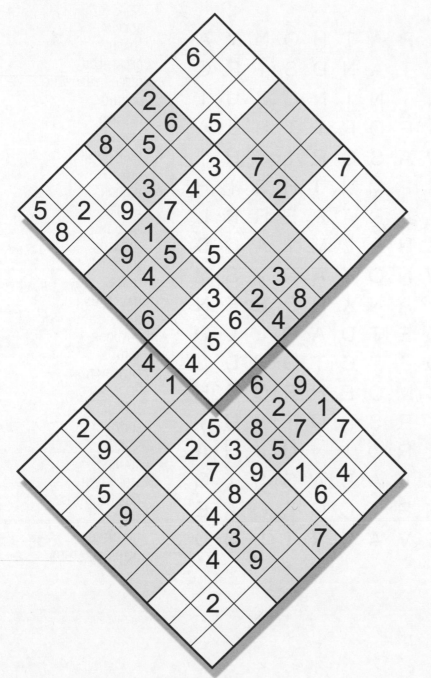

★ Athletics

All the words are hidden vertically, horizontally or diagonally, both forward and backward. The letters that remain unused form a sentence from left to right.

```
U L T R A M A R A T H O N Y A
T H E L E T S T A N D S I R C
D S R C T R A I N I N G S U I
I H S O A A S P O R T T H J A
S O S T O R W A S O R I G N I
C E N T D D Y P M U J H G I H
U S A N O I T A R A P E R P L
S L D Y P P C U L L M I A O S
T P N E I L W N O E A N V S Y
H O I L N I I A N K R D E E N
R D W K G L K E T D A O L L O
O I L T E C O J T C T O H D L
W U I V A S B M O E H R G R H
I M A R C O I R S H O T P U T
N J T O E L E R O I N U J H A
G E A B E K C L A S W S S I C
C C K O L Y M P I C G E O A E
H A M E S G E V A E R T L N D
```

BOEBKA
COACH
DECATHLON
DISCUS-THROWING
DOPING
GEVAERT
GRAVEL
HIGH JUMP
HURDLES
INDOOR
INJURY
JAVELIN
JOHNSON
JUNIOR
LEWIS
MARATHON
MILE
OUTDOOR
PODIUM
PREPARATION
RELAY RACE
SHOES
SHOT PUT
SPIKES
STANDS
STOPWATCH
TAIL WIND
TRACK
TRAINING
ULTRAMARATHON

IN HARMONY

What do these words have in common?

acceded, baggage, bedface, cabbage, defaced, effaced

★ Word Sudoku

Complete the grid so that each row, each column and each 3 x 3 frame contains the nine letters from the black box below.
The hidden nine-letter word is in the diagonal from top left to bottom right.

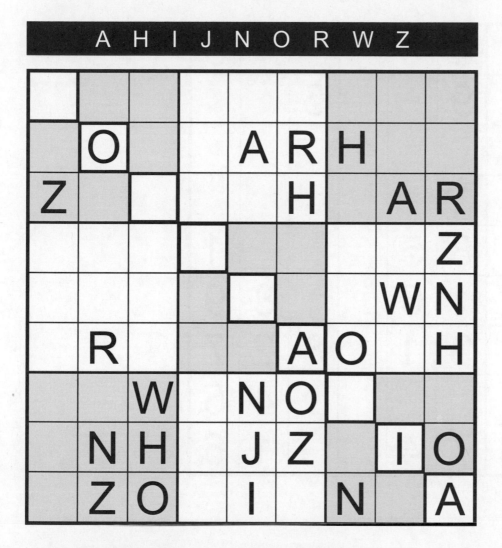

A H I J N O R W Z

THE NUMBER IS THE QUESTION

Which number should replace the question mark?

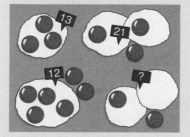

★ Sudoku X

Fill in the grid so that each row, each column and each 3 x 3 frame contains every number from 1 to 9. The two main diagonals of the grid also contain every number from 1 to 9.

			4					8
3			9			5		
					1			
	9		8	5				1
5		2	1	6			8	9
6			3	1		8	2	7
		1					4	5
	5	8	7	4			1	6

TRANSADDITION

Add one letter to I SIT NOT UNTO and rearrange the rest, to create a set of rules.

★★ **Binairo®**

Complete the grid with zeros and ones until there are 6 zeros and 6 ones in every row and every column. No more than two of the same number can be next to or under each other. Rows or columns with exactly the same content are not allowed. There is only one valid solution.

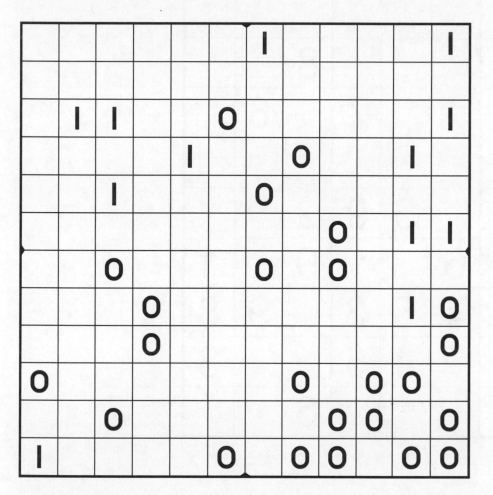

SUMMING UP

Here is a word sum using simple addition. Each letter represents a certain number.
Find this keyword and solve the puzzle by substituting the appropriate numbers for the letters in the sentence below.

```
    T R O U T
  R E F U S E
        T O
    R I S E
      F O R
        M E
  R U U M U U
```

★★ Classic Sudoku

Fill in the grid so that each row, each column and each 3 x 3 frame
contains every number from 1 to 9.

						8		
	4		1		7		6	
5		7						
	1			5	9	2		
		4	6			9		1
		5	4	6	3		9	8
	6			1	5			3
4	3	1				6		

DOUBLETALK

What four-letter word can either mean to advertize or to stop?

★★ Number Cluster

Cubes showing numbers have been placed on the grid below with some spaces left empty. Can you complete the grid by creating runs of the same number and of the same length as the number? So where a cube with number 5 has been included on the grid you need to create a run of five number 5's, including the cube already shown. The run can be horizontal, vertical or both horizontal and vertical.

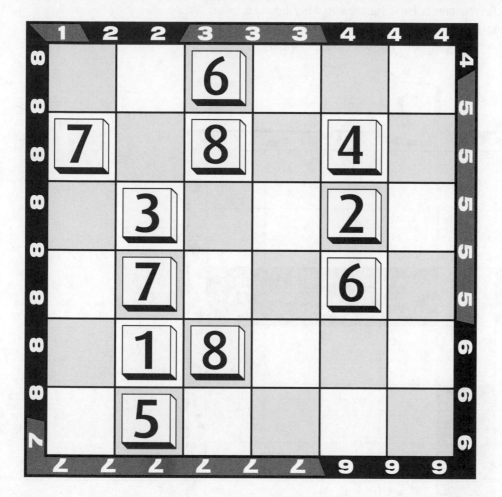

IDIOMATICALLY SPEAKING

Which idiom means "to be the victim of one's own action which was intended to harm someone else"?

★★ Keep Going

Start on a blank square of your choice and connect as many blank squares as possible with one single continuous line. You can only connect squares along vertical and horizontal lines, not along diagonal lines. You must continue the connecting line up until the next obstacle—ie, the rim of the box, a black square or a square that has already been used. You can change directions at any obstacle you meet. Each square can only be used once. The number of blank squares that will be left unused is marked in the upper square. There is more than one solution, but we only show one.

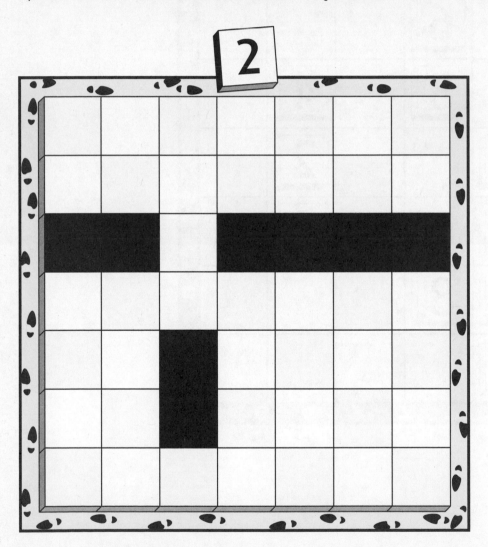

DIARY NOTE

In a year, some months have 31 days, while some have 30. Which month has 28 days?

★★ Binairo®

Complete the grid with zeros and ones until there are 5 zeros and 6 ones in every row and every column. No more than two of the same number can be next to or under each other. Rows or columns with exactly the same content are not allowed. There is only one valid solution.

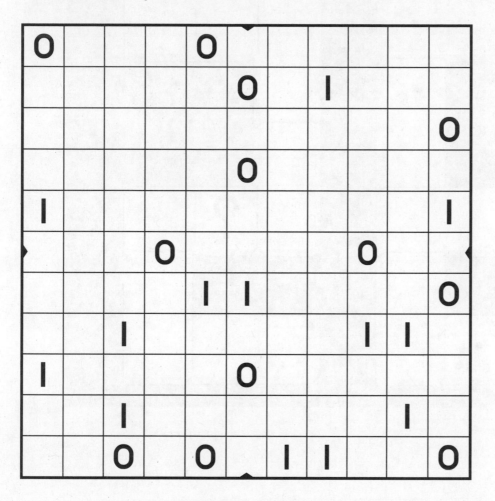

SPEAKING VOLUMES

Bibliolatry is excessive reverence for a book. A bibliophile is a collector of rare books. What do you call a seller of rare books?

★★ Domino Effect

How many dots should replace the question mark on the domino?

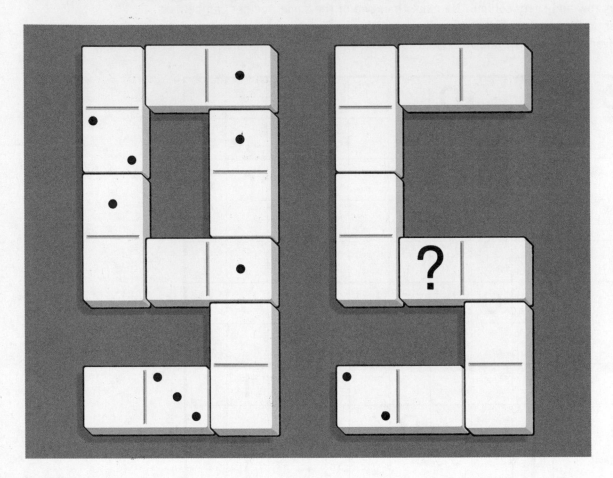

LETTER BLOCKS

Move the letter blocks around so that words are formed on the top and bottom that you can associate with parts of the body.

★★ Sudoku X

Fill in the grid so that each row, each column and each 3 x 3 frame contains every number from 1 to 9. The two main diagonals of the grid must also contain every number from 1 to 9.

								1
				6				
	9		1		4		5	2
		1	8		5		4	3
	8			4				
		9	2	1		7		5
		8	5					
	6	2					9	4
						5		

LONELY WORDS

There are four words in the English language with which no word rhymes. What are they?

★★ Reindeer Games by Karen Peterson

ACROSS

1. 2002 Jason Patric film
5. Postal machine
10. Ed's *Up* role
14. Olive in a Caesar salad?
15. Pianist Claudio
16. Cologne of Bongo-Congo
17. Steven's partner
18. "___ by Me": Ben E. King
19. Crèche trio
20. Diane in *Chinatown*
21. U2 album *Rattle and ___*
22. *Norma* and *Carmen*
24. Flanders river
26. Bed board
27. Hoofer
30. Bigwigs
31. George W. Bush's brother
34. Splashdown site
35. ___ and kin
36. Iditarod Trail end
37. Cary in *Charade*
38. Roman 61
39. Kate Moss, notably
40. Dole (out)
41. Shape with a hammer
42. Bay window
43. Ski wood
44. Celtic woman's homeland
45. TLC givers
46. Extended family
47. Nocturnal insect
48. Apple season
51. Q's Scrabble value
52. Soft touches
56. Call a halt to
57. "You're a Grand Old Flag" composer
59. Leave out
60. Polo in *Little Fockers*
61. Acclimate
62. "Tomb Raider" Croft
63. Monkeyed around?
64. O'Reilly of *M*A*S*H*
65. Linda of *Jekyll & Hyde*

DOWN

1. Josh Groban Christmas album
2. Thomas ___ Edison
3. Clarinet insert
4. Christmas tree hanging
5. Churn plunger
6. Pianist Rubinstein
7. Universal Studios transport
8. Suffix for Mozart
9. Tango dancer Valentino
10. Celestial snowball
11. Feast of Lots month
12. Baltic seaport
13. Redolent garlands
23. Ballet step
25. Mailed
26. Audit a class
27. Church doctrine
28. Homestead Act's 160
29. Below, in verse
30. Female fox
31. Foster in *The Beaver*
32. Kuwaiti royal
33. "Jingle ___"
35. Calvin of fashion
36. Home of Santa's workshop
39. Merely academic
41. High-stepper
44. Majestic tree
45. Pass in the Sierra Nevadas
46. Sam Cooke song
47. Anne in *The Out-of-Towners*
48. *The Thin Man* terrier
49. School near the Rio Grande
50. Lit out
51. Drop heavily
53. *Diary of ___ Housewife* (1970)
54. Makeshift swing
55. Magi guide
58. "Hooked ___ Feeling"

★★ Number Cluster

Cubes showing numbers have been placed on the grid below with some spaces left empty. Can you complete the grid by creating runs of the same number and of the same length as the number? So where a cube with number 5 has been included on the grid you need to create a run of five number 5's, including the cube already shown. The run can be horizontal, vertical or both horizontal and vertical.

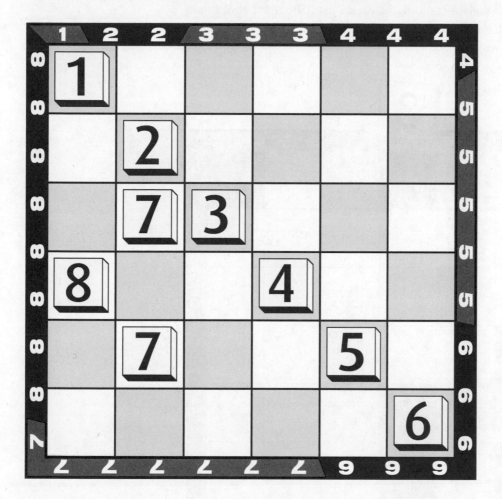

DOUBLETALK

Which four-letter word can mean moving quickly or not able to move at all?

★★ Keep Going

Start on a blank square of your choice and connect as many blank squares as possible with one single continuous line. You can only connect squares along vertical and horizontal lines, not along diagonal lines. You must continue the connecting line up until the next obstacle—ie, the rim of the box, a black square or a square that has already been used. You can change directions at any obstacle you meet. Each square can only be used once. The number of blank squares that will be left unused is marked in the upper square. There is more than one solution, but we only show one.

GREEDY LETTER

Which is the only letter in the alphabet that does not have one syllable, but has three?

★★ Holiday Viewing by Karen Peterson

22 "___ Love You": Beatles
24 Montreal street
25 Leprechaun's lid
27 Baton
28 Jai ___
29 Colleen
31 Genetic carrier
33 Suffix for photo
35 Lang of *Smallville*
36 Enya's homeland
37 "To a Louse" and "To a Mouse"
39 Tattoo word
43 Blunder
45 Tag players, at times
46 Ogres
47 "If" group
48 Luft in *Grease 2*
49 Dark hardwood
51 Justice Kagan
53 Semester
56 Well-heeled
57 Rowling's Madam Pince
58 Frost product
61 Debussy's "Air de ___"

ACROSS
1 NBA team
5 *Aladdin* tiger
10 ___ gratias
13 Place de l'Étoile sight
14 Hirsch in *Milk*
15 ___-chill factor
16 Old money of Rome
17 Cunard ship
18 Abhor
19 Dregs
20 Quiche ingredient
21 Small piano
23 *Torch Song Trilogy* hero
26 Sirius and Spica
27 Furniture wood
30 Spine-tingling
32 Winged
33 First senator in space
34 Staple Singers member
38 Sally Ride's org.
39 Dame Nellie ___
40 No piece of cake
41 Platter
42 *For Your Eyes ___* (1981)
43 Hudson in *Ghostbusters*
44 Ceiling
46 Dennehy and Wilson
47 Sound heard in *Babe*
50 Ted Danson series
52 Healthy
54 Guido's high note
55 Junket
59 Love god
60 Cary in *Twister*
62 Spanish surrealist
63 One of the Brontës
64 Mirthful
65 Pinnacle
66 Calendar square
67 *Apocalypto* subjects
68 Fraud

DOWN
1 *Annie ___* (1977)
2 Lake in HOMES
3 Building lot
4 1994 Tim Allen film
5 Give in
6 Francisco's friend
7 1996 Sinbad film
8 *Cakes and ___*: Maugham
9 ___ *to Hold* (1943)
10 "People's Princess"
11 Enroll
12 *Golden Boy* dramatist
15 1954 Rosemary Clooney film

★★ Word Sudoku

Complete the grid so that each row, each column and each 3 x 3 frame contains the nine letters from the black box below. A hidden nine–letter word is in the diagonal from top left to bottom right.

A C F H I N O T W

	A					T		
					A	I		
			H					
			N			W		
O	W		F		I			
H	N		W			A		
I		N		W			H	
		H		N	O		W	
		O	T		H	C	A	N

SOUND ALIKE

Homophones or homonyms are pairs of words which sound the same but are spelled differently. One of such a pair means to hit or strike; the other is a vegetable. What are they?

★★ Time to Reflect

Draw the two pictures as if they were reflected in the water.

HIDDEN WORDS

My FIRST'S an egotist's delight;
In my NEXT, a vehicle's in sight;
My LAST, you'll find, will make a bed;
My WHOLE'S a story widely read.

★★ Bring Me Sunshine

Where will the sun shine, knowing that each arrow points toward a spot where a symbol should be located? The symbols cannot touch each other vertically, horizontally or diagonally. A symbol cannot be placed on top of an arrow. We show one symbol to start you off.

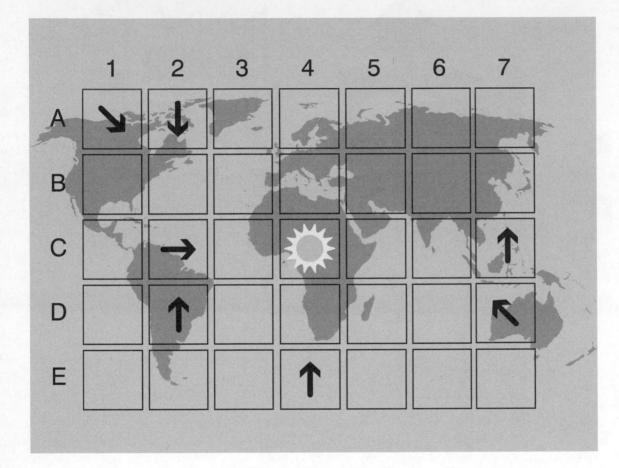

OOPS!

What basic mistake did Shakespeare make in *The Winter's Tale* when he described the infant Perdita as being driven by a storm on the coast of Bohemia?

★★ Sudoku Twin

Fill in the grid so that each row, each column and each 3 x 3 frame contains every number from 1 to 9. A sudoku twin is two connected 9 x 9 sudokus.

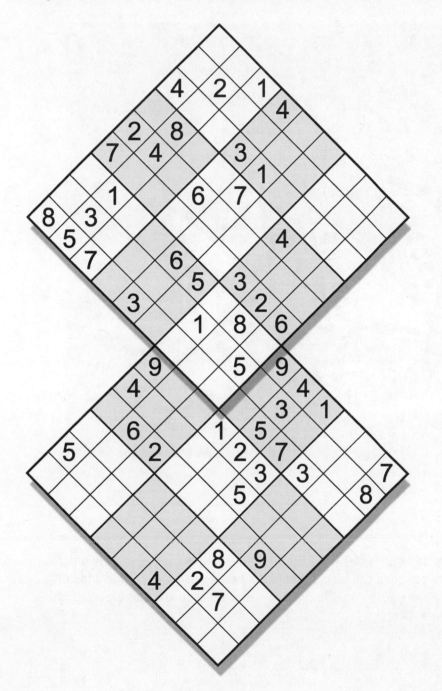

★★ Surf's Up

Surfboards with the same color sail are on the same team. Which surfboard has the wrong contest number?

FIVES AND FOURS

Each line contains a five-letter and four-letter word that have been mixed together (the order of the letters in each word has not been changed). Unmix the two words on each line and write them in the spaces provided. When you're done, find a two-part answer to the clue by reading down the letter columns in the answers.

CLUE: Affection? A good place to land!

HSISTESAM   — — — — —   +   — — — —

COLPEAPRA   — — — — —   +   — — — —

FRLOUGIOT   — — — — —   +   — — — —

TTEOTNEMT   — — — — —   +   — — — —

★★ Number Cluster

Cubes showing numbers have been placed on the grid below with some spaces left empty. Can you complete the grid by creating runs of the same number and of the same length as the number? So where a cube with number 5 has been included on the grid you need to create a run of five number 5's, including the cube already shown. The run can be horizontal, vertical or both horizontal and vertical.

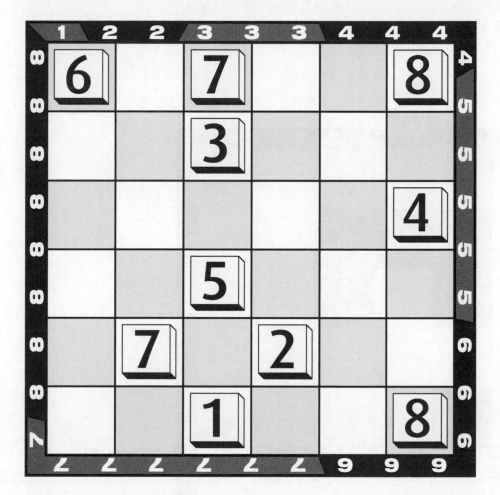

HIDDEN WORDS

Think of the three separate words which, when grouped into one, mean exactly that.

— — — — — — — — —

★★ Keep Going

Start on a blank square of your choice and connect as many blank squares as possible with one single continuous line. You can only connect squares along vertical and horizontal lines, not along diagonal lines. You must continue the connecting line up until the next obstacle—ie, the rim of the box, a black square or a square that has already been used. You can change directions at any obstacle you meet. Each square can only be used once. The number of blank squares that will be left unused is marked in the upper square. There is more than one solution, but we only show one.

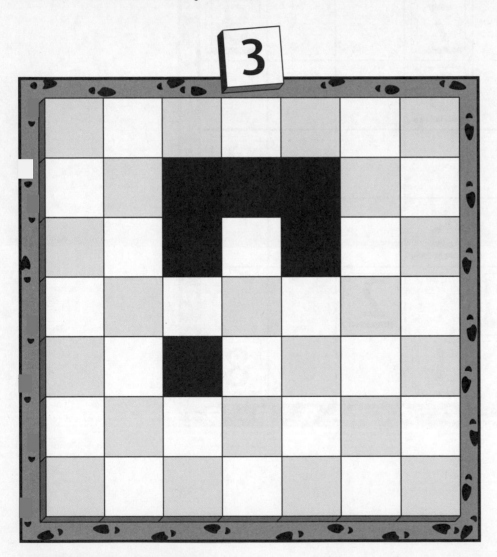

RUNNING REPAIRS

Adding the same letters front and back puts this word back together.

_ _ _ to _ _ _

★★ **Binairo**®

Complete the grid with zeros and ones until there are 6 zeros and 6 ones in every row and every column. No more than two of the same number can be next to or under each other. Rows or columns with exactly the same content are not allowed. There is only one valid solution.

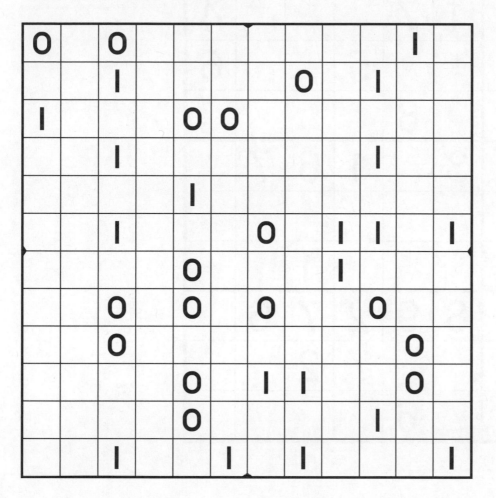

CHANGE ONE

Change one letter in each of the two words, to form a common two-word phrase.
WETTER TRIP

★★ Classic Sudoku

Fill in the grid so that each row, each column and each 3 x 3 frame contains every number from 1 to 9.

3	2	8	1	7				4
		7			5			6
	6			8				
2	5	9	3		1	6	7	
8	1							
	4					1		
			8	9	2	7	6	
					7	2		
			6					

NOT IN ANY STATE

Which letter of the alphabet is the only one not used in the names of any American states?

★★ Kakuro

Each number in a black area is the sum of the numbers that you have to fill in to the next empty boxes. The empty boxes that make up the sum are called a run. The sum of the across run is written above the diagonal in the black area, and the sum of the down run is written below the diagonal. Runs can only contain the numbers 1 through 9, and each number in a run can only be used once. The gray boxes only contain odd numbers and the white only contain even numbers.

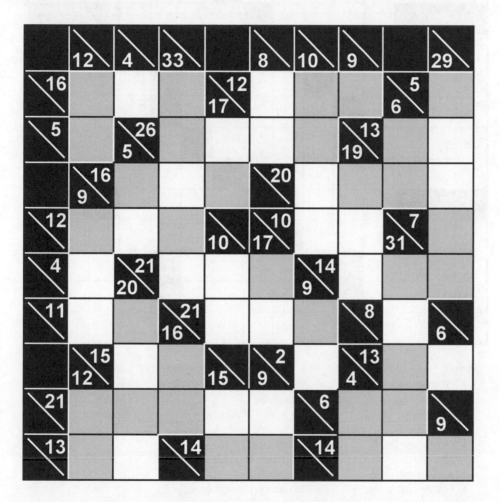

ALL ALONE

Which of these numbers is the odd one out?

82   43   26   50   37   17   5   65

★★ Early TV by Don Law

ACROSS

1 *Essays of Elia* author
5 Up, in a way
10 Sort
14 Dominican baseball family
15 Spar verbally
16 Worked the soil
17 "You don't know the ___ of it!"
18 Come to mind
19 "Good grief!"
20 Embarrassed
22 Former Las Vegas casino
24 Calla lily, for one
25 *Airplane!* autopilot
26 Don't compare these to oranges
29 How William Shatner speaks French
33 Bunch of baby birds
34 ___ of Mexico
35 Put-in-Bay's lake
36 Bumbler
37 "You're shaking like ___"
38 Cry out
39 ___ Domini
40 Paris proms
41 Like Tom Thumb
42 Cormorants, e.g.
44 Infant's shoe
45 B'way hit signs
46 100 centavos
47 Eggnog spice
50 Janet Fitch's *White* ___
54 A case of pins and needles
55 Lace tip
57 Congerlike
58 Jonathan Larson musical
59 Courtroom event
60 "Fancy" singer McEntire
61 Colorful fish
62 Chip away at
63 Stretch across

DOWN

1 "If I Were King of the Forest" singer
2 Maple seeds
3 Jell-O form
4 *The Howdy Doody Show* host
5 Ancient calculator
6 Female seal group
7 *Idylls of the King* character
8 Infomercials
9 Henna, for one
10 Jackie Gleason series
11 Eastern discipline
12 Juicy fruit
13 Icelandic epic
21 "O, My Luve's Like ___ ...": Burns
23 Absorbed, as a cost
25 Cooking pots
26 Palestinian leader Mahmoud
27 Inclined
28 City ESE of Mumbai
29 Coal and peat
30 Milk-Bone, e.g.
31 Charles de Gaulle's birthplace
32 *Safari Disco Club* group
34 Sword lilies, for short
37 Repeal a law
41 Baseball's "Slammin' Sammy"
43 Temper
44 *The Love Bug* bug
46 Beg
47 Franco in *Camelot*
48 BYU rival
49 Charlie, for one
50 Mixed bag
51 Bottomless
52 Island near Corsica
53 Reynolds in *Green Lantern*
56 Doberman warning

★★ Wriggler

Just like in genetics, dominant colors are at play here. Which worm (A–C) should replace the question mark?

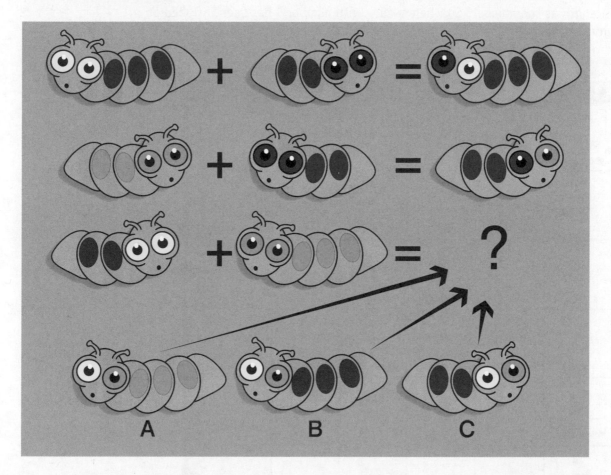

UNCANNY TURN

Rearrange the letters of this word to form a cognate anagram, one which is related or connected in meaning to the original. The answer can be one or more words.
SCHOOLMASTER

★★ Number Cluster

Cubes showing numbers have been placed on the grid below with some spaces left empty. Can you complete the grid by creating runs of the same number and of the same length as the number? So where a cube with number 5 has been included on the grid you need to create a run of five number 5's, including the cube already shown. The run can be horizontal, vertical or both horizontal and vertical.

1	2	2	3	3	3	4	4	4	
8	7	5							4
8									5
8									5
8			1	2					5
8			3	4					5
8	8								6
8	6								6
7	7	7	7	7	7	7	9	9	9	6

IMPORTANT CAPITAL

There is one word which changes from a noun or verb to a nationality when its first letter is capitalized. What word?

★★ Keep Going

Start on a blank square of your choice and connect as many blank squares as possible with one single continuous line. You can only connect squares along vertical and horizontal lines, not along diagonal lines. You must continue the connecting line up until the next obstacle—ie, the rim of the box, a black square or a square that has already been used. You can change directions at any obstacle you meet. Each square can only be used once. The number of blank squares that will be left unused is marked in the upper square—in this case, none. There is more than one solution, but we only show one.

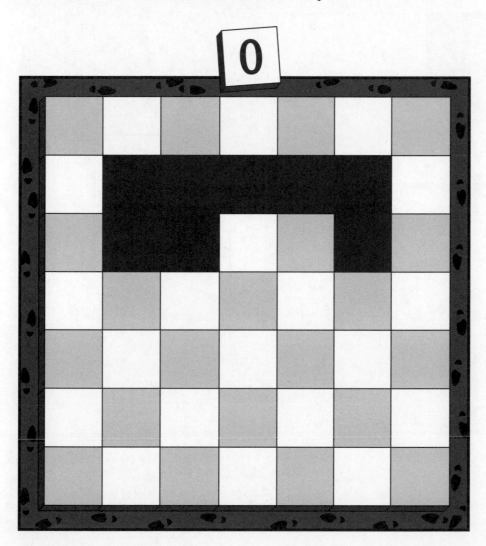

WORD POWER

A collective noun is one which refers to a group of people, animals or things considered as a whole. What is the collective noun for rhinoceroses?

★★ In the Box

Draw the contour of all sides of the inside of this opened cube on the grid.

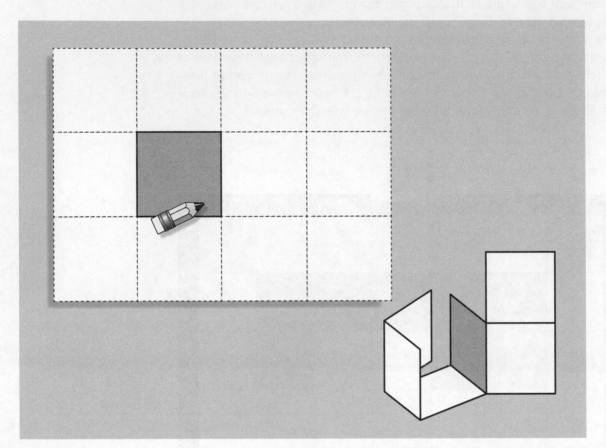

IN REVERSE

Solve the first clue, then reverse your answer to solve the second clue.
Or work in reverse.
i) Grass   ii) Stag or Doe

★★ Bring Me Sunshine

Where will the sun shine, knowing that each arrow points toward a spot where a symbol should be located? The symbols cannot touch each other vertically, horizontally or diagonally. A symbol cannot be placed on top of an arrow. We show one symbol to start you off.

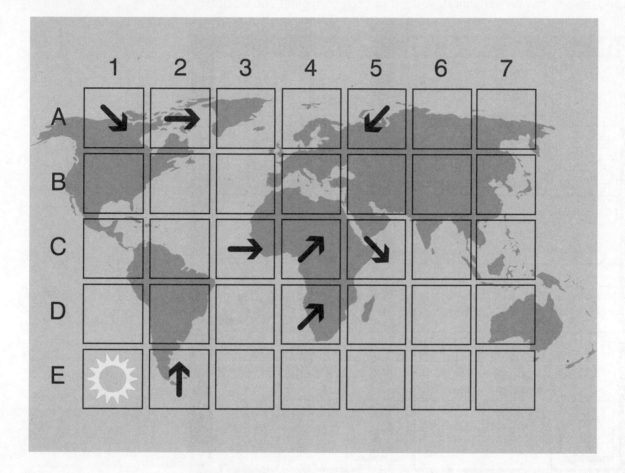

LETTER BLOCKS

Move the letter blocks around so that words are formed on the top and bottom that you can associate with numbers.

★★ Number Cluster

Cubes showing numbers have been placed on the grid below with some spaces left empty. Can you complete the grid by creating runs of the same number and of the same length as the number? So where a cube with number 5 has been included on the grid you need to create a run of five number 5's, including the cube already shown. The run can be horizontal, vertical or both horizontal and vertical.

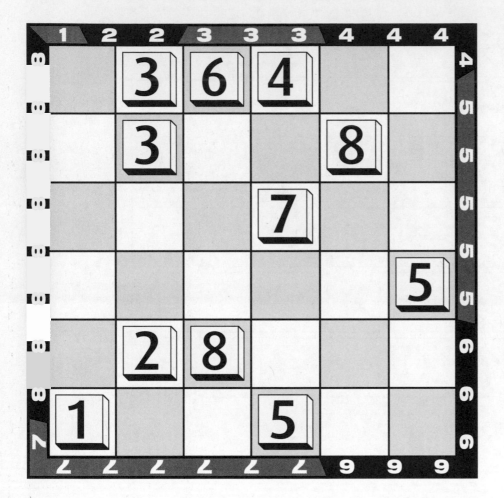

DELETE TWO

Delete two letters from the word ORCHESTRATE and rearrange the rest, to get some pulling power.

★★ Keep Going

Start on a blank square of your choice and connect as many blank squares as possible with one single continuous line. You can only connect squares along vertical and horizontal lines, not along diagonal lines. You must continue the connecting line up until the next obstacle—ie, the rim of the box, a black square or a square that has already been used. You can change directions at any obstacle you meet. Each square can only be used once. The number of blank squares that will be left unused is marked in the upper square—in this case, none. There is more than one solution, but we only show one.

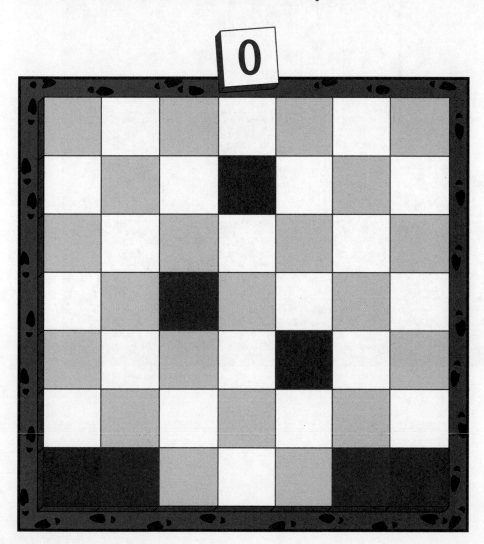

ECONOMICAL

There is only one word that is made using only two different letters, each used three times. What is it?

★★ Hair of the Dog

Two of these drinks (1–6) will definitely give you a hangover. Can you discover which ones, knowing that you will not get a hangover from drinking two good drinks?

AN APPLE A DAY

How can you share two apples between two fathers and two sons, while giving each one a whole apple?

★★ **Binairo**®

Complete the grid with zeros and ones until there are 5 zeros and 6 ones in every row and every column. No more than two of the same number can be next to or under each other. Rows or columns with exactly the same content are not allowed. There is only one valid solution.

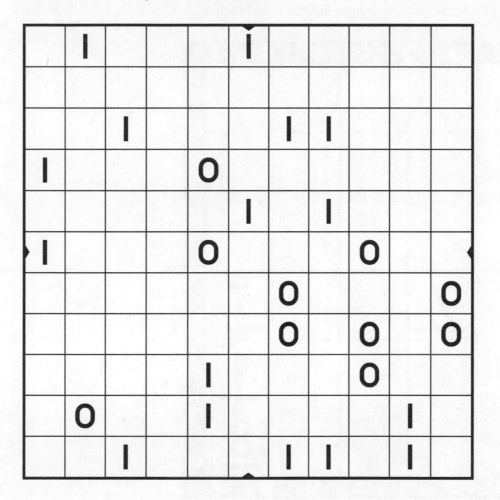

BLOCK ANAGRAM

Form the word that is described between parentheses with the letters above the grid. One or more extra letters are already in the right place.

Declaration   (used to stimulate muscle and bone growth)

★★ Number Cluster

Cubes showing numbers have been placed on the grid below with some spaces left empty. Can you complete the grid by creating runs of the same number and of the same length as the number? So where a cube with number 5 has been included on the grid you need to create a run of five number 5's, including the cube already shown. The run can be horizontal, vertical or both horizontal and vertical.

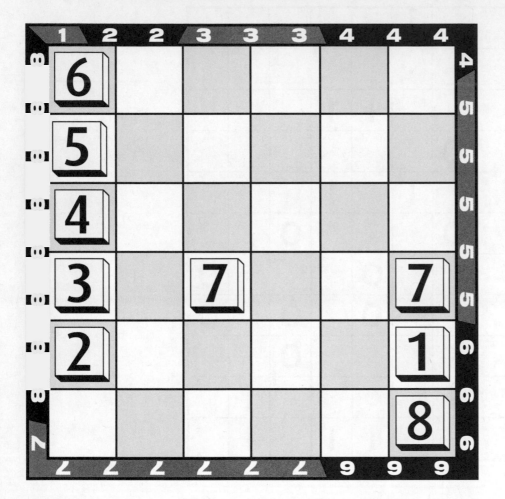

WORKPLACES

Rearrange the letters in the words below to spell out the names of different workers.

LAMENESS   DRIVE   INTERIMS   CHEATER   TERRAIN

★★ Keep Going

Start on a blank square of your choice and connect as many blank squares as possible with one single continuous line. You can only connect squares along vertical and horizontal lines, not along diagonal lines. You must continue the connecting line up until the next obstacle—ie, the rim of the box, a black square or a square that has already been used. You can change directions at any obstacle you meet. Each square can only be used once. The number of blank squares that will be left unused is marked in the upper square. There is more than one solution, but we only show one.

MISSING LETTER PROVERB

Fill in each missing letter, indicated by X, to make a well-known proverb.
XEXNX XIXE PXXNX FXXLXSX.

★★ Inventions by Karen Peterson

ACROSS

1 "Aren't we the comedian!"
5 Gossip blogger Hilton
10 Compos mentis
14 *The Time Machine* race
15 Alpine crest
16 "Home" singer Sheryl
17 Hindmost
18 Concerning color
19 "I loved it!" review
20 Ruth Handler creation
22 Joie de vivre
23 *Two and a Half Men* neighbor
24 "Amazing!"
26 Lumberjack
29 Walter Hunt invention
35 ___ leg (hurry)
37 Toy building block
38 Actress Maryam d'___
39 "Men Working" marker
40 Commandeer
42 Part of UTEP
43 "___ live and breathe!"
44 1/60,000 min.
45 Keanu in *Speed*
47 John Hopps invention
50 McCartney's *Standing ___*
51 ___ *for Gumshoe*: Grafton
52 *Broadway, My Way* singer Linda
54 ___ *'em High* (1967)
57 Arthur Sicard invention
63 Telltale sign
64 Aegean Sea region
65 Give a hoot
66 Herman Melville book
67 Senior Circuit members
68 "What ___ of Fool Am I?"
69 King of Skull Island
70 "No ___ !"
71 Luge

DOWN

1 Saffron, e.g.
2 Epithet of Athena
3 Coating of frost
4 George Westinghouse invention
5 Appetizer spreads
6 Becomes a gully
7 Jean in *The Da Vinci Code*
8 List shortener
9 Renée in *My Own Love Song*
10 Absurdly impractical
11 Shrinking Asian sea
12 A Pacific salmon
13 Bremner in *Pearl Harbor*
21 *Gas Food Lodging* actress Skye
25 Plains tribe
26 Tin Pan Alley org.
27 Nelson Mandela's language
28 Berserk
30 *The Honeymooners* wife
31 Casablanca cap
32 "Flying Finn" Nurmi
33 *A Doll's House* dramatist
34 Lasso loop
36 Stephen Sondheim musical
41 "A cockroach!"
42 Fads conceived by Gary Dahl
44 Romanized *Space Odyssey* year
46 German donkey
48 New Year's drink
49 Upgrade circuitry
53 Wayne Ratliff creation
54 Ring punch
55 Rounds
56 "On tap" sign, sometimes
58 ___ *me tangere*
59 Doozy
60 Cry
61 Maritime eagle
62 Foxx who was Sanford

★★ Double Dutch

What is the translation of symbol 1?

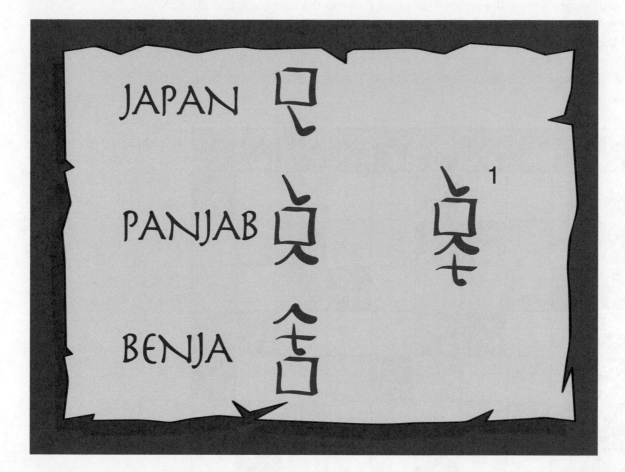

FIRST THINGS FIRST

Identify the first line of a famous Irish blessing from the first letters in each of its words, without its capital vowels.

M. T. R. R. T. M.

★★ Kakuro

Each number in a black area is the sum of the numbers that you have to fill in to the next empty boxes. The empty boxes that make up the sum are called a run. The sum of the across run is written above the diagonal in the black area, and the sum of the down run is written below the diagonal. Runs can only contain the numbers 1 through 9, and each number in a run can only be used once. The gray boxes only contain odd numbers and the white only contain even numbers.

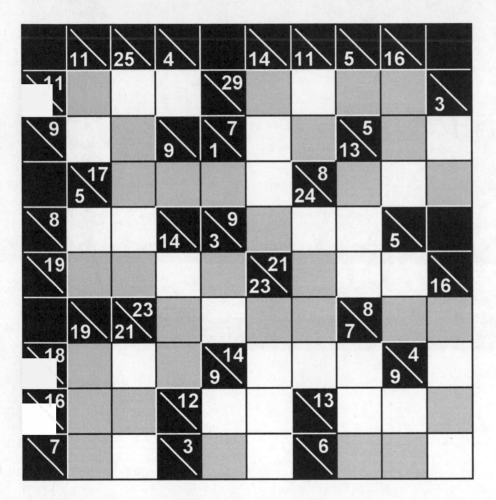

SHOWROOM SHUFFLE

A car dealer found that he did not have enough space for eight new cars which were due to be delivered. So he increased his showroom by one half, and then found that he had room for eight more than his whole number.

How many cars did he have when the eight cars arrived?

★★ Bond Girls by Tim Wagner

ACROSS

1 Bowler
4 Kon-Tiki wood
9 After-game meeting place
12 Ottoman chieftain
14 Steer clear of
15 "Come in and ___ spell"
16 Club for Els
17 "Like ___, all tears ...": Hamlet
18 Org. for Saudi Arabia
19 *Octopussy* actress
21 First Hebrew letter
22 *A Day Without ___*: Enya
23 *CSI* evidence
24 Offer evidence
27 *Casino Royale* actress
32 Anchor's concern
33 Gets in the game
34 "C'est la ___!"
35 Catch on
37 Tread the boards
38 Buy and sell
40 " ___tu": Verdi aria
41 Kalahari stopover
43 Overmedicated
44 *Diamonds Are Forever* actress
46 Ashes-to-be
48 100 qintars
49 *Mikado* blade
50 "Employee of the Month," e.g.
53 *On Her Majesty's Secret Service* actress
58 Ex of Tiger Woods
59 Deep Nevada lake
60 Belmonte's bull
61 Lana of *Smallville*
62 Milicevic in *Casino Royale*
63 Graceful bird
64 Henna, for one
65 Bowed out
66 "Yes, Captain!"

DOWN

1 *License to Drive* star Corey
2 India tourist site
3 "How Great ___ Art"
4 Highwayman
5 Like some sanctuaries
6 Materialize
7 A boy and his sis
8 Juice drink
9 Corncob ___
10 Lone Star State college
11 "Art of the Fugue" composer
13 Ursula in *Dr. No*
15 Green energy
20 Remote batteries
21 High anxiety
23 "___ Tripper": Beatles
24 Illusionist Criss
25 ___ cotta
26 "Up" singer Shania
27 11th-century Spanish hero
28 Brewery containers
29 Duck the issue
30 Downy duck
31 Musts
33 ___ doble (Spanish dance)
36 Potency
39 Julia in *Ocean's Twelve*
42 "All systems go!"
45 "___ came a spider ..."
46 Group of 52 Down
47 "Cry ___ River"
49 Lyon river
50 Grasped
51 A skin moisturizer
52 Three times three
53 ___ Matthews Band
54 "If ___ a nickel for ..."
55 Davenport's place
56 Squirrel color
57 Left
59 Twitch

★★ Classic Sudoku

Fill in the grid so that each row, each column and each 3 x 3 frame contains every number from 1 to 9.

			7					
								2
				9			3	
		8			1	2		6
	2		5			3		
	1			6	8			
9	5	4	1		7		2	
7	6				2	1	5	
2			6		3			9

DON'T BE FLOORED!

A do-it-yourself enthusiast was laying a wooden floor. But coming close to the end of the job, he realized that he needed an exact square to finish it off. All he had left was a piece of wood this shape, so he decided to saw it up so that, with two straight cuts, he would form a perfect square with the three pieces. How did he do it?

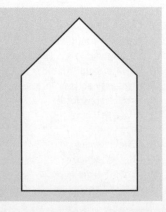

★★ Spaced Out

Which electron orbit (A–E) is configured incorrectly?

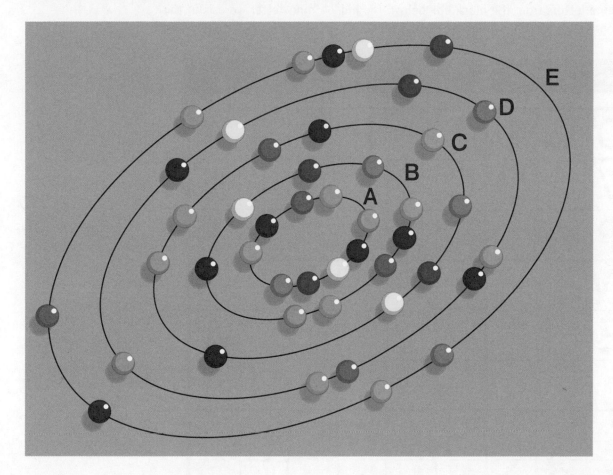

CHANGE ONE

Change one letter in each of the two words, to form a common two-word phrase.
SLAY PAT

★★ Word Sudoku

Complete the grid so that each row, each column and each 3 x 3 frame contains the nine letters from the black box below. The hidden nine–letter word is in the diagonal from top left to bottom right.

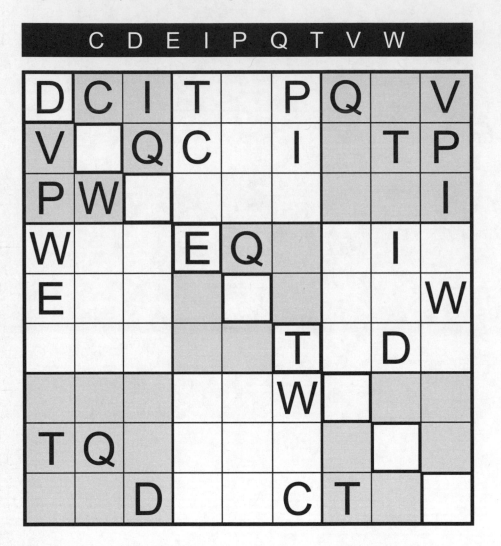

C D E I P Q T V W

SANDWICH

What five-letter word belongs between the word at left and the word at right, so that the first and second word, and the second and third word, each form a common compound word?

TIME _ _ _ _ _ WORK

★ Number Cluster

Cubes showing numbers have been placed on the grid below with some spaces left empty. Can you complete the grid by creating runs of the same number and of the same length as the number? So where a cube with number 5 has been included on the grid you need to create a run of five number 5's, including the cube already shown. The run can be horizontal, vertical or both horizontal and vertical.

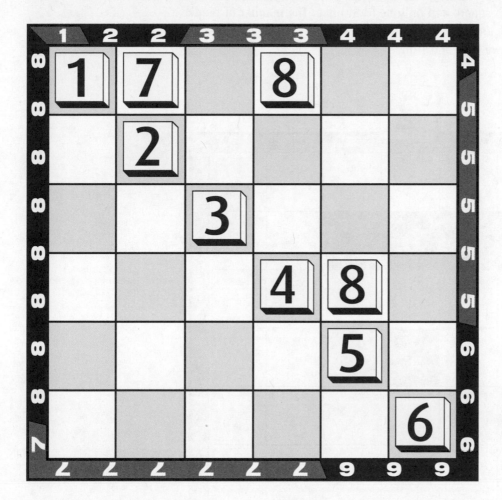

FRIENDS?

What do the following words have in common?
　　GROWTH　CHARGE　SIGNED　PASSES　SCORED　HAND　STAND

★★ Keep Going

Start on a blank square of your choice and connect as many blank squares as possible with one single continuous line. You can only connect squares along vertical and horizontal lines, not along diagonal lines. You must continue the connecting line up until the next obstacle—ie, the rim of the box, a black square or a square that has already been used. You can change directions at any obstacle you meet. Each square can only be used once. The number of blank squares that will be left unused is marked in the upper square. There is more than one solution, but we only show one.

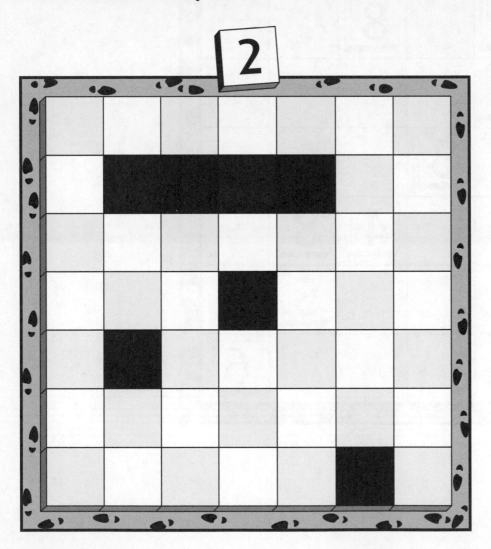

FIRST THINGS FIRST

Identify the well-known proverb from the first letters of each of its words.
T. W. F. N. M.

★★ Sudoku Twin

Fill in the grid so that each row, each column and each 3 x 3 frame contains every number from 1 to 9. A sudoku twin is two connected 9 x 9 sudokus.

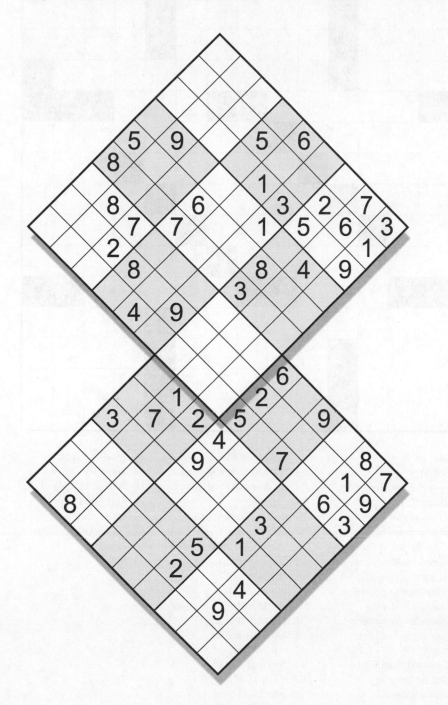

★★ Bond Villains by Tim Wagner

ACROSS

1 Jackman in *Australia*
5 Elite Navy team
10 *Enterprise* journey
14 Ending for buck
15 Shoelace tag
16 "Hava Nagila" dance
17 Vibraphonist Jackson
18 Gloomy, to poets
19 Piece of cake
20 Roman 2,550
21 *Casino Royale* villain
23 ___ mignon
25 Watering hole
26 *A Few Good Men* director
28 Avenger's action
33 Building wing
34 Wherewithal
35 Roman 401
36 Crying binges
37 "Key to the city" presenter
38 Dodge trucks
39 Noshed
40 Of the ear
41 Javier ___ de Cuéllar
42 *Fiddler* actor Bernardi
44 Afloat
45 Big Band ___
46 "Haste makes waste" is one
47 *The Spy Who Loved Me* villain
51 Sumac effect
54 Trudge
55 Deadly African snake
56 Birthplace of Ceres
57 Golden prefix
58 Mueller-Stahl in *Shine*
59 *Ghostbusters* character
60 Bond villain Julius
61 Dora the Explorer's cousin
62 Bromides

DOWN

1 *Toy Story* pig
2 ___ and Thummim
3 Oddjob's boss
4 Crisis center connection
5 "The Ballad of the Green Berets" singer
6 Long-legged bird
7 Trevelyan in *GoldenEye*
8 Jacob's first wife
9 Bachelor party dancer
10 "Most Wanted" list org.
11 Greeting from Simba
12 Dublin language
13 *Eloise* author Thompson
22 Ferocity
24 Clark's *Smallville* friend
26 Princess Jasmine's pet
27 Related maternally
28 Imperial
29 Hydroxyl compound
30 *The Man With the Golden Gun* villain
31 Blurb specialists
32 "Liebestraum" composer
34 Stable mate
37 Founder of Islam
38 AARP members
40 Height: Comb. form
41 Peace goddess
43 *A Fistful of Dollars* director Leone
44 1998 Olympics site
46 *Live and Let Die* villain
47 Insulting remark
48 Ripped
49 Port of SE Italy
50 Aare tributary
52 White stuff
53 "Gladiator" composer Zimmer
54 Blue

★★ **Follow the Line**

Try to draw this shape with one continuous line without lifting your pencil off the page and without overlapping.

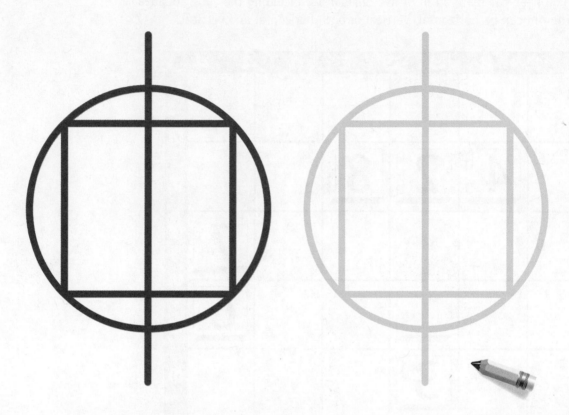

SANDWICH

What five-letter word belongs between the word at left and the word at right, so that the first and second word, and the second and third word, each form a common compound word?

POWER _ _ _ _ _ BOATS

★★ Number Cluster

Cubes showing numbers have been placed on the grid below with some spaces left empty. Can you complete the grid by creating runs of the same number and of the same length as the number? So where a cube with number 5 has been included on the grid you need to create a run of five number 5's, including the cube already shown. The run can be horizontal, vertical or both horizontal and vertical.

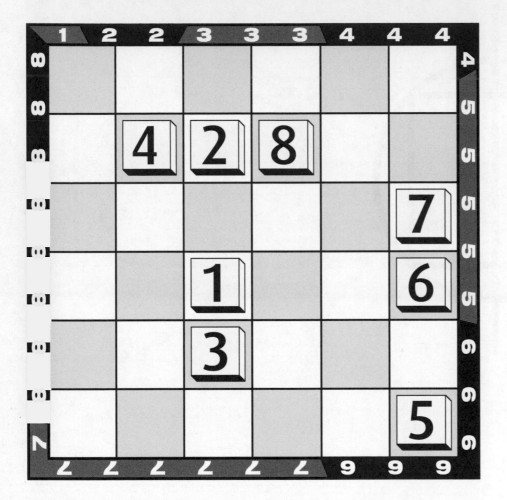

BLOCK ANAGRAM

Form the word that is described between parentheses with the letters above the grid. One or more extra letters are already in the right place.

Bracelet   (decreases force and rate of heart contractions)

★★ Winner's Circle by John McCarthy

ACROSS
1 Wolverine player Jackman
5 *Buffy the Vampire Slayer* villain
10 Jell-O form
14 Building lot size
15 Green lizard
16 Certain facial oil
17 Snowboarded
18 Mariner's friend in *Waterworld*
19 "Me Tarzan, you ___"
20 Ache of a sort
21 2010 Kentucky Derby winner
23 Window stick-on
25 LII doubled
26 Womanizer
28 Flushes out game birds
33 Acclaim
34 Gaiters
35 Penultimate Greek letter
36 Drain problem
37 1955 Kentucky Derby winner
38 ___ moss
39 1,200 months: Abbr.
40 *The Wreck of the Mary ___*: Innes
41 Beatnik drum
42 Sufficient
44 Arboretum
45 In toto
46 ___ Rica
47 1983 Kentucky Derby winner
52 Diamond stats
55 Harness gait
56 Zeroed (in on)
57 German car
58 Turner in *Peyton Place*
59 Customary
60 *Rhyme Pays* rapper
61 Hispanic hurrahs
62 *Waiting to Exhale* novelist McMillan
63 Some George Foreman wins

DOWN
1 A padlock may pass through it
2 *Daily Bruin* publisher
3 1996 Kentucky Derby winner
4 Porcupine
5 Romaine salad
6 Abolish
7 Aerial maneuver
8 *Allure* competitor
9 Classic Stutz models
10 Las Vegas desert
11 Patron saint of Norway
12 Wisteria of *Desperate Housewives*
13 Batik artisan
22 Letter opener
24 *Cinderella* frame
26 Birthplace of Muhammad
27 Connected, as wheels
28 Fifth tire
29 Zorro's wear
30 1985 Kentucky Derby winner
31 Accepted practice
32 Spike for Everest
34 Smack
37 Close tightly
38 "Mona Lisa," for one
40 Properly
41 ___-relief
43 "Flying Kangaroo" airline
44 Considerable
46 See-through
47 Normandy battle site
48 Eurasian mountains
49 Not a lick
50 Hydrant attachment
51 Manchurian border river
53 Word form of "thought"
54 Assumes a reading position

★★ Stormy Weather

Where will the storms be, knowing that each arrow points to a spot where a symbol should be located? The symbols cannot touch each other vertically, horizontally or diagonally. A symbol cannot be placed on top of an arrow. We show one symbol to start you off.

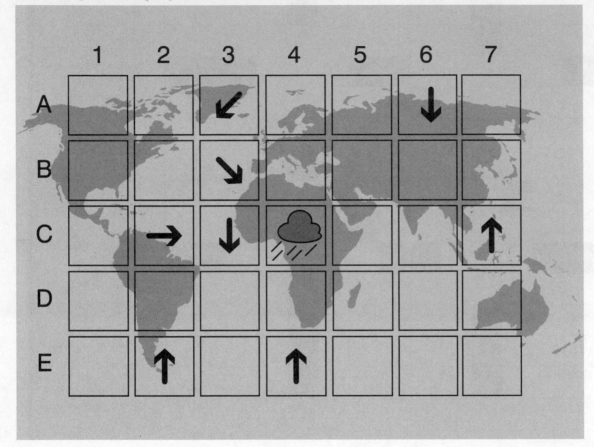

TRANSADDITION

Add one letter to NO TIMID FACTIONS and rearrange the rest to find a V.I.P.

★★ Kakuro

Each number in a black area is the sum of the numbers that you have to fill in to the next empty boxes. The empty boxes that make up the sum are called a run. The sum of the across run is written above the diagonal in the black area, and the sum of the down run is written below the diagonal. Runs can only contain the numbers 1 through 9, and each number in a run can only be used once. The gray boxes only contain odd numbers and the white only contain even numbers.

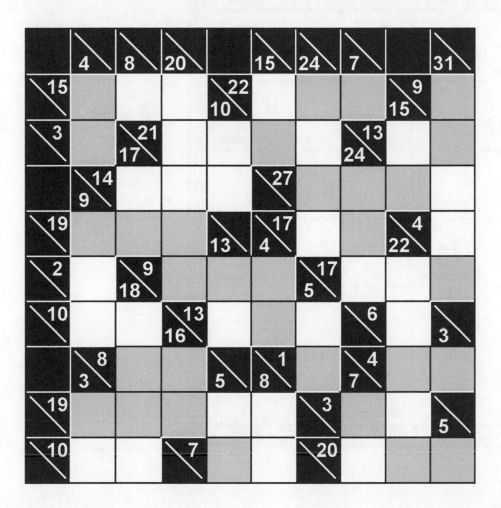

ANAGRAM

Unscramble the letters in the phrase BATTERED SPORRANS to form four words with the same or similar meanings.

★★ Number Cluster

Cubes showing numbers have been placed on the grid below with some spaces left empty. Can you complete the gird by creating runs of the same number and of the same length as the number? So where a cube with number 5 has been included on the grid you need to create a run of five number 5's, including the cube already shown. The run can be horizontal, vertical or both horizontal and vertical.

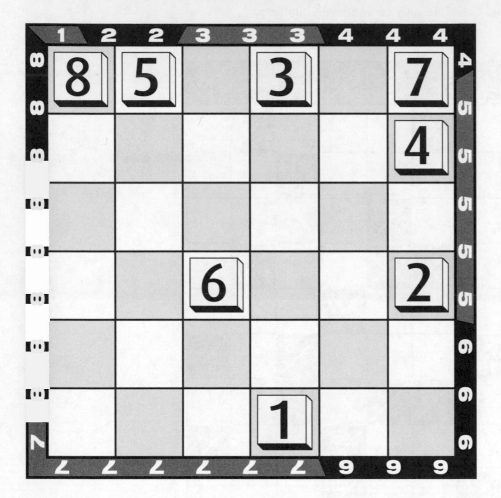

UNCANNY TURN

Rearrange the letters of this phrase to form a cognate anagram, one which is related or connected in meaning to the original. The answer can be one or more words.
   SLOT MACHINES

★★ Cubed
Which piece (1–6) completes the cube?

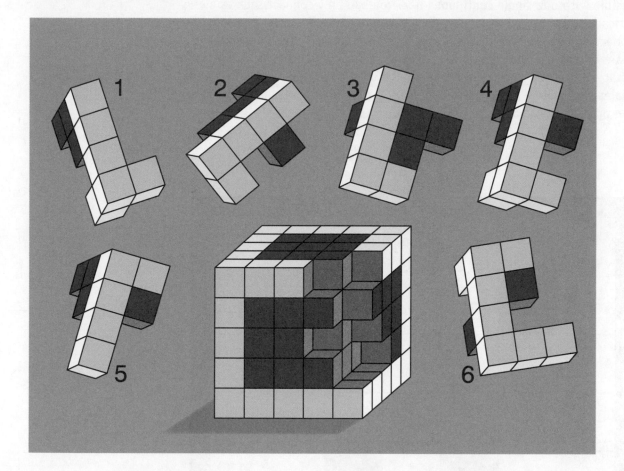

INHERITANCE TEST

A family had a piece of land. It was decided that a will would be made so that the two sons and two daughters would each inherit equal amounts of land of similar shape. The triangular part had already been sold to a developer. How was the land shared?

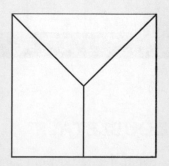

★★ Keep Going

Start on a blank square of your choice and connect as many blank squares as possible with one single continuous line. You can only connect squares along vertical and horizontal lines, not along diagonal lines. You must continue the connecting line up until the next obstacle—ie, the rim of the box, a black square or a square that has already been used. You can change directions at any obstacle you meet. Each square can only be used once. The number of blank squares that will be left unused is marked in the upper square. There is more than one solution, but we only show one.

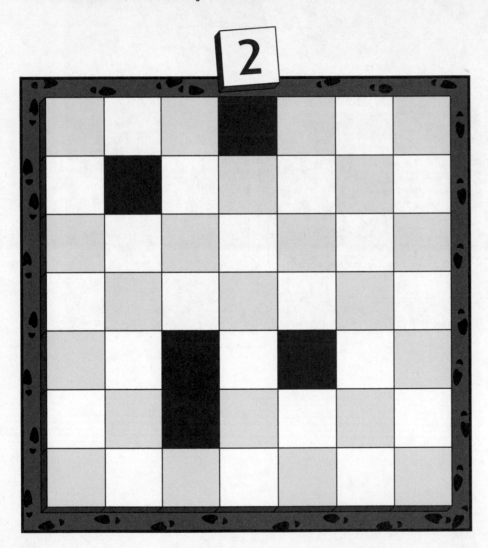

DOUBLETALK

What five-letter word can either mean part of a tree, or to stab?

★★ Kakuro

Each number in a black area is the sum of the numbers that you have to fill in to the next empty boxes. The empty boxes that make up the sum are called a run. The sum of the across run is written above the diagonal in the black area, and the sum of the down run is written below the diagonal. Runs can only contain the numbers 1 through 9, and each number in a run can only be used once. The gray boxes only contain odd numbers and the white only contain even numbers.

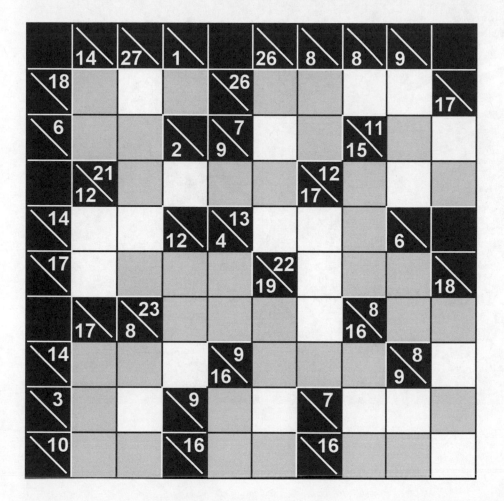

BLOCK ANAGRAM

Form the word that is described between parentheses with the letters above the grid. One or more extra letters are already in the right place.

Morons (secretion of an endocrine gland)

★★ Party Time

Where (1–6) is the item that is located across from the item that is 3 places counterclockwise from the item that is across from the item to the left of the champagne cork?

DELETE ONE

Delete one letter from each of these words and rearrange the rest to come up with the answer.
SOON   SUN   TOIL

★★ Augusta Winners by Tim Wagner

10 Cookie Monster's street
11 Room-service item
12 Ford SUV
13 Former *Tonight Show* host
22 Do dock work
24 Dryly amusing
26 Elsie the Cow's hubby
27 *Lorna* ___
28 Osprey nest
29 Drano target
30 1998 Masters winner
31 "Consider it done"
32 Bowed out
34 Sloop or dory
37 Belgian capital
38 Nullified a marriage
40 French Open court surface
41 Gold of *Entourage*
43 Syracuse U. team
44 Stick like glue
46 Flirtatious one
47 "Come" or "go"
48 Skating star Kulik
49 XK cars, for short
50 "Not folding"
51 *The Godfather* composer Rota
53 "FOR SALE," e.g.
54 Aphrodite's son

ACROSS
1 "No ___ allowed"
5 A cappella composition
10 "Bake at 375° for 15 minutes," e.g.
14 Freshwater mussel
15 Heep in *David Copperfield*
16 *Das Rheingold* contralto
17 Far from peppy
18 Ganders
19 *Beowulf* or *Iliad*
20 Academy freshman
21 1978 Masters winner
23 Tied another knot
25 Hasty escape
26 Prince Harry's uncle
28 Theoretical
33 Bananas
34 Disprove
35 Dazzle
36 Cattle calls
37 Atomic number 5
38 Adjective for Death Valley
39 Conclude
40 Daniel in *Quantum of Solace*
41 "Twisted" body part
42 Determined
44 1964 Masters winner Palmer
45 "Dorm police," so to speak
46 Deep dislike
47 2000 Masters winner
52 ___ majesté
55 Dash
56 *Nana* author Zola
57 Cougar cave
58 *Evil Under the Sun* actress Diana
59 Royal Caribbean ship
60 "And so ..."
61 Headquarters
62 "Are you asleep?" response
63 Aykroyd and Fogelberg

DOWN
1 Orange-juice option
2 Organic compound
3 2005 Masters winner
4 Protein-rich legumes
5 Made a face
6 Attendant to Artemis
7 Stadium section
8 A cinch
9 "The rain in Spain falls mainly on ___"

★★ TOP-RANKED by Don Law

ACROSS

1 "Regrets only" alternative
5 Breakfast sizzler
10 Hooked-bill bird
14 Cerebral passage
15 Military march
16 Jacob's twin
17 "I Remember It Well" musical
18 Lukewarm
19 Statesman Gingrich
20 Be drawn toward
22 Frost lines
23 Bouquet
24 Norm for Norman
25 Star in Gemini
28 Alaskan sled-dog race
33 "I Love a Parade" composer
34 About
35 *Blazing Saddles* heroine
36 Chick's sound
37 Staples Center hoopster
38 "The Merry Drinker" painter
39 Nonpareil
40 "Bejabbers!"
41 "America's Drive-In"
42 He met his Waterloo
44 Butters up
45 ___ for Peril: Grafton
46 Clutch
48 Clean up, in a way
51 "Mrs. Robinson" songwriter
55 Bring up baby
56 Prize money
57 Whitewall
58 Brooklyn Bridge river
59 Levitated
60 Green car in *Cars 2*
61 "See how ___ run ..."
62 Sing like Bing
63 Advance

DOWN

1 *Evil Under the Sun* actress Diana
2 Ruckus
3 Bright star in Lyra
4 "NO TRESPASSING"
5 Mandalay Bay whale
6 Elite squad
7 Friend of Mr. Green Jeans
8 *The Andy Griffith Show* lad
9 Homer's TV neighbor
10 Where Luke married Laura
11 ___-friendly
12 Parts of a code
13 Minstrel's instrument
21 Club for David Toms
22 Big wine holder
24 Marina feature

25 Roasting fowl
26 Sports venue
27 Forty winks
29 Harriet Beecher Stowe book
30 Cheery
31 Stan's costar in *Swiss Miss*
32 Platters
34 Parrot in *Aladdin*
37 Dregs
41 Act saucy
43 A boxer might have a fat one
44 Whalebone
47 Rene in *Get Shorty*
48 Bart Maverick's brother
49 Remini on *The King of Queens*
50 Fluency

51 Feline sound
52 Unwanted house guests
53 Ishii of *Kill Bill* films
54 Doofus
56 Lobbying group

★★★ Sport Maze

Draw the shortest way from the golf ball to the hole. You can only move along vertical and horizontal lines, not along diagonal lines. The number on each square indicates the number of squares the ball must be moved in the same direction. You can change directions at each stop.

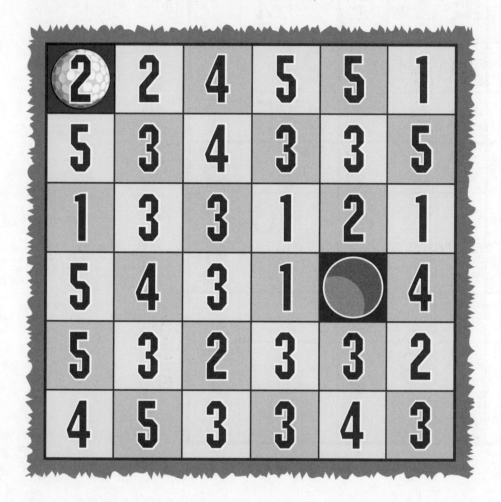

SOUND ALIKE

Homophones or homonyms are pairs of words which sound the same but are spelled differently. One of such a pair is audible; the other, permitted. What are the words?

★★★ Classic Sudoku

Fill in the grid so that each row, each column and each 3 x 3 frame contains every number from 1 to 9.

			5				4	
		9	3			2		
2			9			1	5	
	3		6			5		8
	9				8		6	
	1							3
4		8			5			
			7	9				

DOODLER

A doodle puzzle is a combination of images, letters and numbers that stands for a word or concept. If you cannot solve a doodle puzzle, do not look at the answer right away. Try to solve it later or tomorrow. When you know the answer, study the puzzle to understand how it works. Explaining doodle puzzles to friends will also reinforce your comprehension.

★★★ Kakuro

Each number in a black area is the sum of the numbers that you have to fill in to the next empty boxes. The empty boxes that make up the sum are called a run. The sum of the across run is written above the diagonal in the black area, and the sum of the down run is written below the diagonal. Runs can only contain the numbers 1 through 9, and each number in a run can only be used once. The gray boxes only contain odd numbers and the white only contain even numbers.

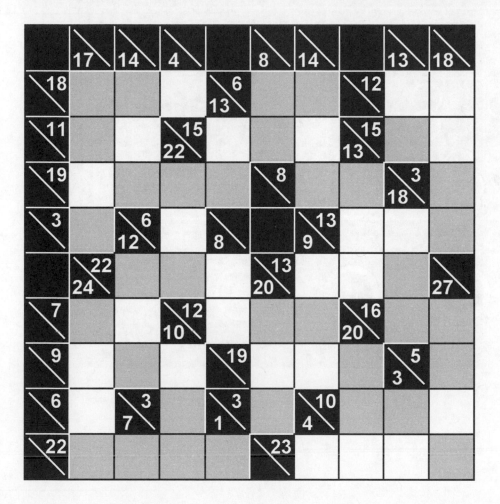

DOUBLETALK

What four-letter word can either mean part of a car, or to cover?

★★★ Place Your Bets

On which number will the player place the next four tokens (2 x A, 1 B and 1 C),
knowing that the three kinds of tokens (A–C) each have a different value?

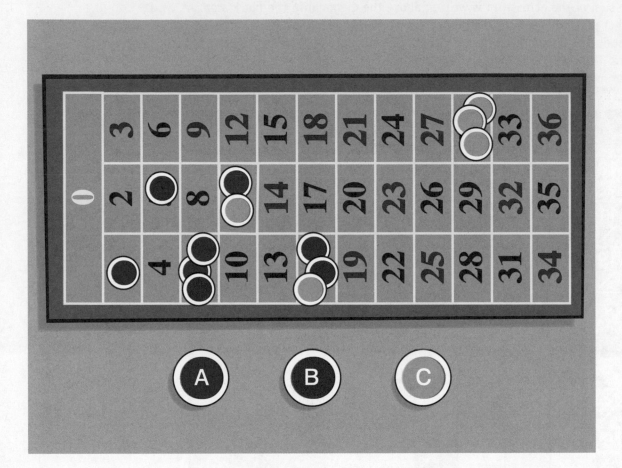

IS IT RIGHT?

Which of these four words is misspelled?

A) unnatural   B) unobtrusive

C) unprecedented   D) unprincipaled

★★★ The Wet Set by Michele Sayer

18 Work as a garçon
22 Acoustic
24 Indian Ocean archipelago
26 Shake up
27 Brochette
28 4-H Club sponsor: Abbr.
29 "Loverboy" singer
30 Classify
34 Out
36 Falco of *Nurse Jackie*
37 Handle
39 Marry cheaply
41 Stomach soother
44 Brynner in *Taras Bulba*
46 Lady of "la casa"
49 Banquet
51 "I Ain't Got ___": Williams
52 Thrashes
53 Roués
54 Flourless cake
58 ___ *Jury*: Spillane
60 Took the train
61 Norman locale: Abbr.
62 River to the North Sea
64 Petrol
65 Wise to

ACROSS
1 Henry VIII's sixth
5 Appeared
10 Aerobic gait
13 Hatred
15 Campus group
16 Conquistador's cache
17 Legendary blues singer (1915–1983)
19 Rhine feeder
20 Cordoba coin
21 Before
22 ___ Christum
23 Thin wedge
25 Bound by oath
27 Amount so far
31 Rani's robe
32 Chi follower
33 Gannet
35 "Nevermore" bird
38 Loaf

40 Big wheel
42 Helen of Troy's mother
43 Sum
45 Himalayan humanoids?
47 Periphery
48 "None of ___ business!"
50 Permit holder
52 Tear
55 Billionth: Comb. form
56 Marathon
57 Hawaiian dish
59 Scotch-and-vermouth cocktail
63 Oahu music maker
64 "Wild Horses" singer
66 Arthur in *Maude*
67 ___ *World Turns*
68 Confuse
69 Taxpayer's ID: Abbr.

70 Submerge
71 It's 88 days on Mercury

DOWN
1 Magnificence
2 Together, musically
3 Eliminates
4 Most impolite
5 Hard-rock links
6 Learning method
7 *Ernani* is one
8 Makes coleslaw
9 Car finish?
10 *The Celebrity Apprentice 2* winner
11 Address the multitude
12 Like some Pamplona runners
14 Legendry

★★★ U.S. History by Karen Peterson

ACROSS

1 Fancy-schmancy
5 *Hardball* network
10 Headless cabbage
14 Eye layer
15 "That's ___ excuse for ..."
16 In the thick of
17 Vice President in 1804
18 Engine booster
19 Off-white
20 U.S. President who spoke Dutch
23 Derek Jeter, for one
24 ___ Kan
25 Apian groups
28 *You've Got* ___ (1998)
30 The woman yonder
33 The ends of the earth
34 *True Grit* star
36 Urbi et ___
37 Aristae
38 Chef's wear
39 Subject of an 1857 Supreme Court decision
41 First U.S. President to marry in office
42 Cyclone center
43 Grow faint
44 With kindness
45 *For Me and My* ___
46 Irish ___ bread
47 U.S. President from New Hampshire
54 Composer Schifrin
55 Gold medalists, often
56 Like Granny Smith apples
58 "___ my wit's end"
59 Hardy in *A Chump at Oxford*
60 Friend of Coleridge
61 *High Noon* hero Will
62 ___-foot oil
63 "Take Me Or Leave Me" musical

DOWN

1 Tavern
2 Egg
3 "Buona ___" (Italian greeting)
4 Nevada statesman
5 Morning prayer
6 Mettle
7 NFL coach Turner
8 ___ Fett (*Star Wars* bounty hunter)
9 Former CBS anchor
10 Afghanistan capital
11 Cupid
12 Ancestry
13 First lady's garden
21 Flat hats
22 Like old tires
25 English potter
26 Brood
27 *Seascape* playwright
28 Unglossy finish
29 Rat-___ (drumbeat)
30 The Joker's expression
31 "___ California" (Eagles hit)
32 Gateway
34 "Are you putting ___?"
35 First Family member in 1980
37 Salad ingredient
40 Love letters?
41 Almanac topic
44 Auditory assaults
45 Yard
46 Banana ___
47 Hopper's nemesis
48 Vishnu incarnate
49 Mathematician Turing
50 Do nothing
51 Spike Lee heroine
52 NASCAR legend Yarborough
53 The Old Sod
57 Make a doily

★★★ Binairo®

Complete the grid with zeros and ones until there are 6 zeros and 6 ones in every row and every column. No more than two of the same number can be next to or under each other. Rows or columns with exactly the same content are not allowed. There is only one valid solution.

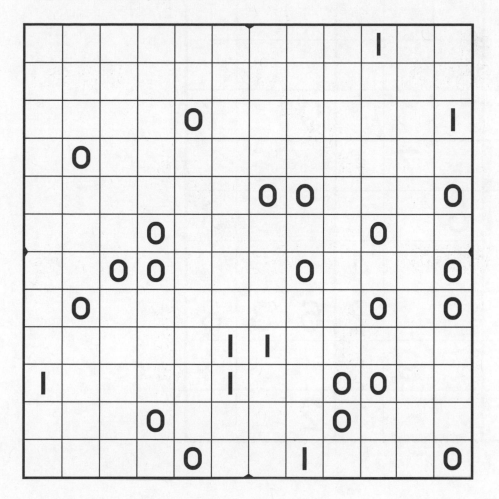

CHANGE ONE

Change one letter in each of these two words, to form a common two-word phrase.
GRAIN TRAIN

★★★ Classic Sudoku

Fill in the grid so that each row, each column and each 3 x 3 frame contains every number from 1 to 9.

		3						
	4							
				1		9		7
		1		7			5	
		7	8					3
					4			
9					2	6	3	8
	6			9				4
5					1	2		

BLOCK ANAGRAM

Form the word that is described between parentheses with the letters above the grid.

Sunni Li   *(accelerates oxidation of sugar in cells)*

★★★ Sport Maze

Draw the shortest way from the golf ball to the hole. You can only move along vertical and horizontal lines, not along diagonal lines. The number on each square indicates the number of squares the ball must be moved in the same direction. You can change directions at each stop.

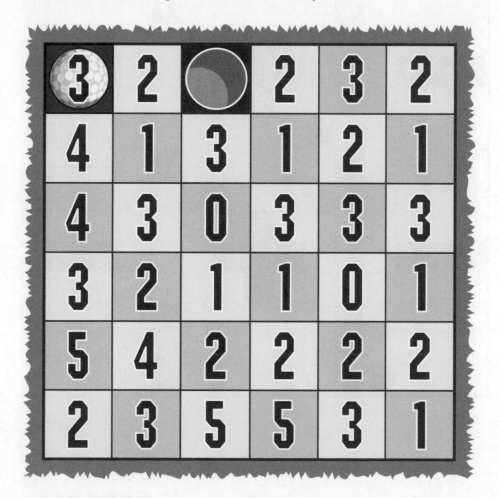

DOODLER

A doodle puzzle is a combination of images, letters and numbers that stands for a word or concept. If you cannot solve a doodle puzzle, do not look at the answer right away. Try to solve it later or tomorrow. When you know the answer, study the puzzle to understand how it works. Explaining doodle puzzles to friends will also reinforce your comprehension.

\W/ΔV

★★★ Oscar Winners by Chris Peterson

ACROSS

1 Rowlands in *Hope Floats*
5 Thumper's friend
10 "His Master's Voice" co.
13 *The Good Earth* heroine
14 Matriculate
15 Virtuous
16 *Schindler's ___* (1993)
17 Conductor Doráti
18 1970 Paul Newman film
19 *Faith of Our ___*
21 Favorite of Scrooge
23 "___ bodkins!"
24 A Bobbsey twin
25 *Weekend at ___* (1989)
29 Edgar Allan Poe poem
33 Daisy that's a weed
34 King's Plymouth Fury
36 Merit-badge holder
37 Saint of baseball
38 Mandlikova of tennis
39 Oscar-winning Elizabeth Taylor film
41 Vernal month
42 Leave for a while
43 "Bam!" chef Emeril
45 "Plop" preceder
46 Salon goo
47 Great Red Spot planet
51 "___ in the Air": Don McLean
55 Pianist Feinberg
56 Dunn and Charles
58 Razzed
59 D.C. team
60 Puzzle parts
61 Olive genus
62 Some dashes
63 "Maybe, Yes" singer Mandell
64 *What Women ___* (2000)

DOWN

1 Sawgrass sport
2 *Baby Doll* director Kazan
3 GOP Elephant creator
4 *The Silence of the Lambs* Oscar winner
5 Amanda of *Married... With Children*
6 Murray and Beattie
7 "Pity the fool!" guy
8 Venice transportation
9 Monopoly avenue
10 One-sided victory
11 "___ fan tutte": Mozart
12 Singer Lambert
15 *Shakespeare in Love* Oscar winner
20 Warhol companion Sedgwick
22 Slangy negatives
25 Autumn pears
26 Raise on high
27 View anew
28 Caan of *Hawaii Five-O*
29 *Perry Mason* event
30 They're unbelievable
31 *Brokeback Mountain* hero
32 Football great "Greasy"
35 Lew Wallace's *Ben-___*
37 Fishburne in *The Matrix Revolutions*
40 Cecil Day Lewis, e.g.
41 *Rock of ___*
44 1992 Wimbledon winner
47 "Fascination" singer Morgan
48 Polish lancer
49 Butter squares
50 Shoot dice
51 Normandy city
52 Johnson in *A Prairie Home Companion*
53 Garden snake locale?
54 Do an usher's job
57 *Golden Girl* McClanahan

★★★ Presidential Runners by Tim Wagner

DOWN
1 Internet column
2 Home-care employee
3 Singer Laine
4 First Family of 1889
5 Downey or Kennedy
6 San Antonio landmark
7 "You Sang to Me" singer Anthony
8 Hose woe
9 Elections have been won by this
10 Small part for a big star
11 Purim month
12 Stretched out
13 "___ I Want to Do": Sugarland
21 Tiny pest
22 Stout
25 Anthrax antibiotic
26 Cinema name
27 Son of Zeus and Europa
28 Part of WHO
29 Eight, in Paris
30 "___ where they ain't": Willie Keeler
31 Like extra-inning games
32 Lip cosmetic
34 Canine command
35 HBO's *Real Time with* ___
37 Portuguese city
40 Aaron of *Thank You for Smoking*
41 Bibliophile's love
44 Heading
45 Bruin on the field
46 Attack times
47 Siesta preceder
48 Fisher in *Wedding Crashers*
49 She, in Cherbourg
50 Faithful
51 *South Park* kid
52 Thumb-twiddling
53 Easter ___
54 Recipe abbr.

ACROSS
1 "Brandenburg Concertos" composer
5 Super Bowl XXXIV winners
9 Lake Tuscawilla locale
14 Snoopy's original owner
15 Buck heroine
16 Spanish tennis star
17 River that joins the Neisse
18 Theda of silents
19 AOL message
20 He ran against Richard Nixon in 1972
23 *Netsuke* container
24 Spirit's shout
25 Communications satellite
28 Give an edge to
30 Fertility drug
33 Kurosawa's *The ___*
34 Boehner may try to pass it
36 Sean in *The Tree of Life*
37 Like a Bigfoot encounter
38 Langston Hughes poem
39 He ran for president four times
41 Endow with talent
42 Add-___ (extras)
43 How vichyssoise is served
44 Hannity's former debater
45 Kiev locale: Abbr.
46 Gloom's partner
47 He ran against George Bush in 1988
54 Palo Alto car company
55 *Maude* producer
56 Jekyll's alter ego
57 Turkic people of China
58 Installs carpeting
59 Scat singer Fitzgerald
60 Herbivore's snack
61 Where starter
62 Projectionist's unit

★★★ Binairo®

Complete the grid with zeros and ones until there are 5 zeros and 6 ones in
every row and every column. No more than two of the same number can be next
to or under each other. Rows or columns with exactly the same content are not
allowed. There is only one valid solution.

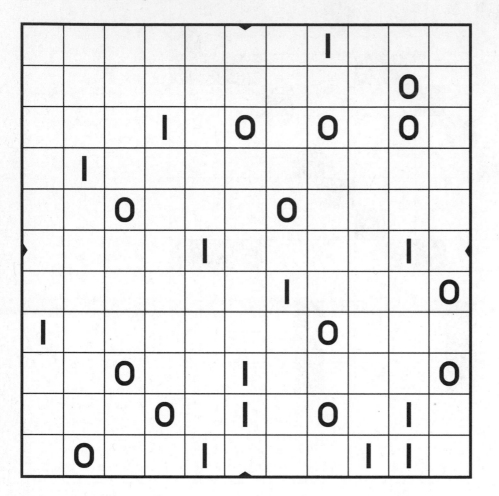

MAGIC SQUARE

In this square, each row, column or diagonal totals 34. There are many
ways that sets of four squares can total 34—for example, 4-1-16-13,
4-15-9-6, etc. How many can you find?

4	15	14	1
9	6	7	12
5	10	11	8
16	3	2	13

★★★ Word Sudoku

Complete the grid so that each row, each column and each 3 x 3 frame contains the nine letters from the black box below. The hidden nine-letter word is in the diagonal from top left to bottom right.

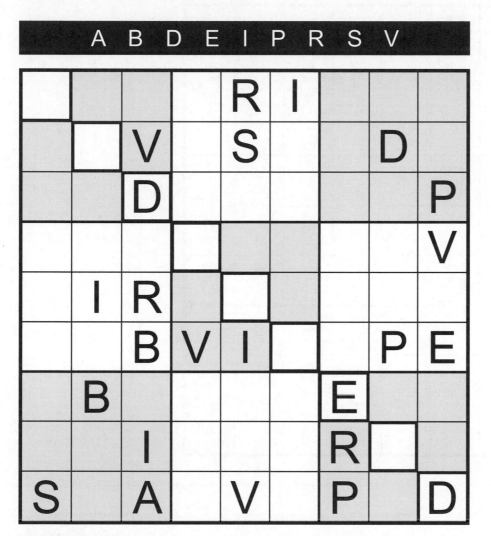

A B D E I P R S V

DOODLER

A doodle puzzle is a combination of images, letters and numbers that stands for a word or concept. If you cannot solve a doodle puzzle, do not look at the answer right away. Try to solve it later or tomorrow. When you know the answer, study the puzzle to understand how it works. Explaining doodle puzzles to friends will also reinforce your comprehension.

SP
―――
SOR

★★★ Sudoku X

Fill in the grid so that each row, each column and each 3 x 3 frame contains every number from 1 to 9. The two main diagonals of the grid must also contain every number from 1 to 9.

	7	5	8					9
			7		1	3		6
				9				
5	6	1	9	3				
								4
7			6					5
6	5							
		4				8		
						1		

SQUARE LINKS

The top horizontal line, indicated by circles, represents an eight-letter word which means a spring flower. Find this word and fill in the remaining spaces so as to form a word square in each half of the diagram.

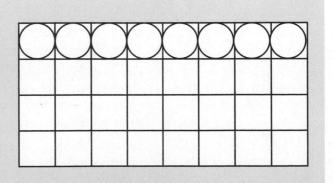

★★★ Hizzoner by Michele Sayer

18 Belgian battlefield of WWI
22 Nightmarish street
23 Christmas tree
24 Iago's wife
25 San Francisco mayor in 2010
26 Monica of tennis
27 Poet Whitman
29 New Orleans mayor in 2009
30 Tranquilize
31 Mouthed off
33 Ex-NYC mayor Dinkins
36 Pasty
37 Aquarium bubblers
39 *A Fistful of ___* (1964)
40 Like Robin Hood's men
42 Sandra in *Gidget*
43 Milwaukee slugger
45 Tylenol rival
46 Grand Cherokee, for one
47 Mode in *The Incredibles*
48 Like dust bowls
51 Cotton knot
52 Caesar's 506
53 Motor City union
54 Rajon Rondo's org.
55 Pink Panther, e.g.

ACROSS

1 Water dogs
5 Shinbones
11 Catherine Bell series
14 Tasteless
15 Go to extremes
16 Oaxaca "whoopee!"
17 New York City mayor in 1926
19 Luke Skywalker's friend
20 Bids first
21 Use a thurible
23 Irish oath
26 "Super!"
28 Bowls over
29 Close call
32 Coward's *Private ___*
33 Dawdle
34 Teachers' union
35 Avoided a tag
36 Debra in *Love Me Tender*
37 Tots up
38 Rhone tributary
39 Tennis cup
40 Badlands scenery
41 Troubadour instrument
43 Tongue-lash
44 Caught congers
45 Decked out
46 "Do You Want To Play" singer
48 At the ready
49 Mayor Koch et al.
50 Atlanta mayor in 1989
56 Ambient music pioneer
57 Resuscitate
58 *Hurlyburly* playwright
59 *The Office* receptionist
60 Arachnid
61 Dog-paddled

DOWN

1 JFK's successor
2 Jerry Quarry's 1970 opponent
3 Emeril's shout
4 Chatted
5 Skyline sights
6 Eric Trump's mom
7 Loudness units
8 Tick off
9 Picnic drink
10 Black magic
11 New York City mayor in 1973
12 "Oh, dear!"
13 Mapping subject

★★★ Sport Maze

Draw the shortest way from the golf ball to the hole. You can only move along vertical and horizontal lines, not along diagonal lines. The number on each square indicates the number of squares the ball must be moved in the same direction. You can change directions at each stop.

4 (ball)	2	3	4	5	1
3	(hole)	2	3	2	4
4	3	2	1	4	5
2	3	2	3	1	1
1	1	1	3	2	2
1	5	4	3	1	3

BLOCK ANAGRAM

Form the word that is described between parentheses with the letters above the grid. One or more extra letters are already in the right place.

BAR DANCER (Someone who uses a divining rod)

	H			O	M				

★★★ Mystery Letter

Which letter block should replace the question mark?

SECURITY PATROL

A security guard and his dog have to patrol the outside of 6 factory buildings, going completely around each building, ten times a night. What is their shortest route?

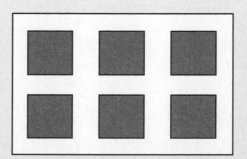

★★★ Kakuro

Each number in a black area is the sum of the numbers that you have to fill in to the next empty boxes. The empty boxes that make up the sum are called a run. The sum of the across run is written above the diagonal in the black area, and the sum of the down run is written below the diagonal. Runs can only contain the numbers 1 through 9, and each number in a run can only be used once. The gray boxes only contain odd numbers and the white only contain even numbers.

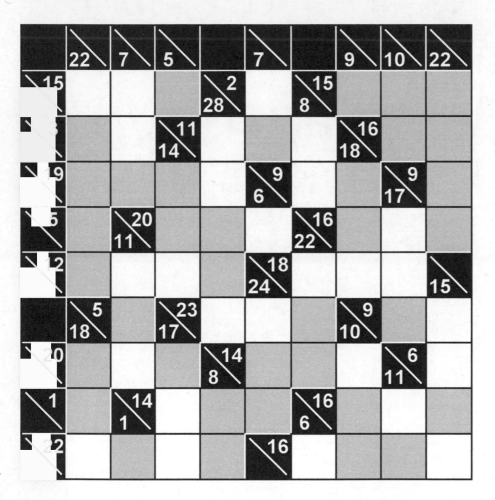

MISSING LETTER PROVERB

Fill in each missing letter, indicated by X, to make a well-known proverb.
PXSSXXXIXN XS NXXX XOIXXS OX XHX XAX.

★★★ Classic Sudoku

Fill in the grid so that each row, each column and each 3 x 3 frame contains every number from 1 to 9.

		7	2		9		8	6
8		6		3				9
		2					3	
9				5	6			
			9	7	4	5		
	1							
	8		4	6				
						3	6	7

LETTER LINE

Put a letter in each of the squares below to make a word which means "cheerful." These numbered clues refer to other words which can be made from the whole: 841 PASSAGE 762 NOTHING 57613 BIRD

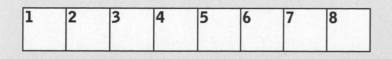

1	2	3	4	5	6	7	8

★★★ Men of Letters by Michele Sayer

ACROSS

1 Half a Hawaiian fish
5 Sleepy, e.g.
10 Way off
14 Jordan of Jordan-Marsh
15 Harder to come by
16 Angler's delight
17 *The Forsyte Saga* author
19 Doe beau
20 In la-la land
21 Oil-can letters
22 Poet Pound
23 New Mexican ski spot
25 Render a verdict
27 Annex
30 Paris streets
32 Satisfy
33 *The Matrix* hero
34 Runway
36 Pierre's thank-you
39 Part of YWCA
41 Khartoum locale
43 Nobleman
44 Giant
46 Excellence
48 Floral necklace
49 Mesabi yield
51 Ten: Comb. form
52 *A Summer Place* star
53 Palate cleanser
56 Short satire
58 ___ Scotia
59 Activate
61 Bolivian beasts
65 Little helper?
66 "The Necklace" author
68 Small dog
69 Goodbye, Gabrielle
70 Goodbye, Reginald
71 Comes out with
72 Dweebs
73 Radiate

DOWN

1 Lotsa
2 "___ le Roi!": Bastille cry
3 *Mutiny on the Bounty* co-author
4 Map feature
5 Quitters
6 Realm of Mars
7 Knacks
8 Detox center
9 Young chickens
10 No-show
11 *The Last Tycoon* author
12 Video-game name
13 Shakespearean princess
18 Dons
24 Vaccine
26 "___ Woman": Reddy
27 Physical-therapy subj.
28 He loved Lucy
29 *The Brothers Karamazov* author
31 Did a vinyl house job
35 Prunes
37 Summer on TV
38 Nastase of tennis
40 Recounts
42 Golden Bear of golf
45 Tortoise beak
47 Monkey suit
50 Deckhand
53 Loses it
54 Biblical prophet
55 FTC concern
57 Liking
60 Sierra Club founder John
62 Drawled address
63 Con
64 RN's "at once!"
67 Foot: Comb. form

★★★ State Mottos by Don Law

23 Part of NATO
24 "He who transplanted sustains" state
25 Gnat
26 Went to pot?
27 Pope in 682
28 Colorado Rockies field
29 Princess Leia's dad
30 Grafton's *N Is for* ___
31 Fort Knox bar
32 Newspaper column
34 Citadel student
37 Subject of a 1990 Ken Burns documentary
41 Where to see "The Last Supper"
43 IOU segment
44 Caprice
46 Noodlehead
47 Like some cellars
48 Not aweather
49 Honolulu Zoo bird
50 Anthem starter
51 Compact Chevy pickup
52 Sonneteer
53 Hathaway in *Get Smart*
56 Chicken ___ king
57 Class rank fig.

ACROSS

1 Cartoonist MacNelly
5 Sings like Ella
10 Caroline of *Sabrina, the Teenage Witch*
14 "It's ___!"
15 Fencing thrust
16 Maul
17 "I have found it!" state
19 Merely
20 *The Spanish Tragedy* dramatist
21 Exchange allowance
22 Gil of baseball
24 "See you, Pasquale!"
25 Supplemental
26 State U. in Lorman, Mississippi
29 "Thus always to tyrants" state
33 Times Square lights
34 Scoundrels
35 Ditty
36 Bluto or Pluto
37 Bum
38 Letterhead symbol
39 Birthplace of Yeats
40 Pierre's notion
41 James in *The Blue Max*
42 Visa rival
44 North Pole's latitude
45 Gibe at
46 Hawked
47 Radcliffe or Craig
50 Twice tetra-
51 Jacuzzi
54 Baldwin of *30 Rock*
55 "By and by" state
58 Carte
59 San Antonio shrine
60 Hammer head
61 Amanda in *Syriana*
62 Cellulose fabric
63 Prefix for room

DOWN

1 Hill climber of rhyme
2 PayPal parent
3 Crease
4 Murphy Brown's show
5 Catchphrase
6 Flea-market item
7 12 *mesi*
8 ___ Friday's
9 Aquarium favorite
10 "Hope" state
11 Put up drapes
12 A.A. Fair's real first name
13 Irving and Grant
18 Blue-ribbon events

★★★ Sport Maze

Draw the shortest way from the golf ball to the hole. You can only move along vertical and horizontal lines, not along diagonal lines. The number on each square indicates the number of squares the ball must be moved in the same direction. You can change directions at each stop.

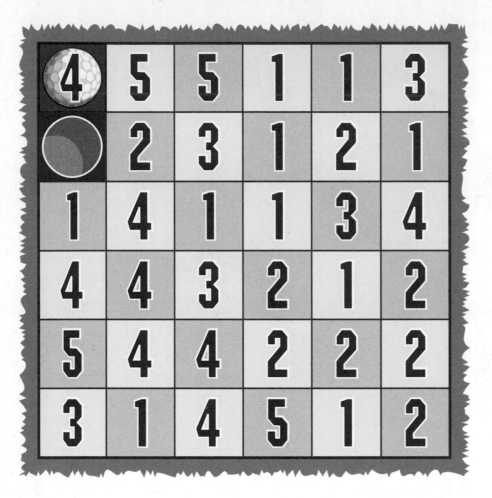

A TIDY ORCHARD

A man wanted to plant 21 fruit trees in a new orchard, so there would be nine straight rows with five trees in each row. The outline of the whole had to be a regular geometric shape. How did he do it?

★★★ Binairo®

Complete the grid with zeros and ones until there are 6 zeros and 6 ones in every row and every column. No more than two of the same number can be next to or under each other. Rows or columns with exactly the same content are not allowed. There is only one valid solution.

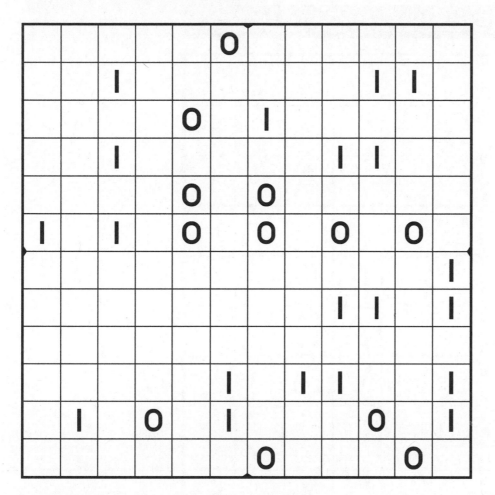

SQUARE LINKS

The top horizontal line, indicated by circles, represents a six-letter word meaning a children's outdoor toy. Find this word and fill in the remaining spaces so as to form a word square in each half of the diagram.

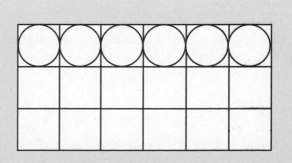

★★★ Word Sudoku

Complete the grid so that each row, each column and each 3 x 3 frame contains the nine letters from the black box below. The hidden nine–letter word is in the diagonal from top left to bottom right.

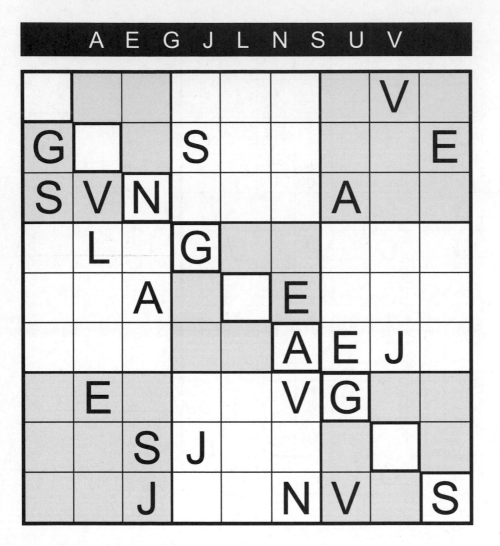

LETTER LINE

Put a letter in each of the squares below to make a word which means "yielded." These numbered clues refer to other words which can be made from the whole:
352 PRONOUN, 85174 GULLED, 651 VESSEL.

1	2	3	4	5	6	7	8

★★★ Themeless by John McCarthy

26 Ancient Persian governor
27 Get some airtime?
28 Keep going
30 *Faust* character
36 Equator's is zero
37 Makes it go
39 Jeff in *Sweet Hearts Dance*
40 Alcohol
45 Loosen a skate
47 Fifty ___ (long odds)
50 What a stitch in time saves
51 *Star Trek* producer Roddenberry
52 Stats at Cooperstown
53 *Mad Men* network
54 ___-jongg
55 Dorm mentors: Abbr.
56 Homey

ACROSS
1 Campaign tactics
8 Went postal
15 Festoon
16 Like pegged pants
17 Allows
18 Backing
19 Breakage
20 Barely flow
21 "Fair!" or "Foul!"
23 Argues logically
26 Flavor
29 Worth a ten
31 "Riddle-me-___" ("Guess!")
32 "And ___ fine fiddle had he"
33 Alternatives to suspenders
34 ___ Aviv
35 Weary

36 Royal reception
37 Beauvais department
38 50 cent piece
39 "Beyond the Sea" singer Bobby
40 ___ *River Anthology*
41 Devoured
42 Angled
43 Al dente order
44 Fragrant flower
46 Hoopla
48 Component
49 Moon color, at times
53 Novice
56 *Guess Who's Coming to Dinner* star
57 "Waltzing ___"
58 Aerial
59 Fontina and Colby
60 Renters

DOWN
1 Added years
2 Blue Nile source
3 Airport conveyance
4 Popular tuna
5 Stampede Park site
6 Use a prayer rug
7 Radical '60s group: Abbr.
8 Matthew and Mark
9 Gross out
10 Takes to a higher court
11 Le Moko and Le Pew
12 Ratio
13 Eternally, in verse
14 *Silent Spring* killer
22 Africa's oldest republic
23 Caves in
24 Liam in *The A-Team*
25 Moon goddess

★★★ A+ Novels by John McCarthy

ACROSS

1 "Please respond"
5 Ranchero's rope
10 Acoma Pueblo is on one
14 Anatomical aqueduct
15 Fire remnant
16 Duck genus
17 Andean land
18 *The Crucible* setting
19 Flood guard
20 E.M. Forster novel
23 Han of *Star Wars*
24 Seine tributary
25 Live
28 Went the full monty
32 Killer whales
33 Billie Holiday's music
34 Always, in verse
35 Cloud seeding result
36 Sombrero features
37 Au naturel
38 Ike's WWII command
39 They all lead to Rome
40 *Andrea* ___
41 Rikki-Tikki-Tavi, for one
43 Globetrotters' home
44 NASDAQ quotes
45 Bang-up
46 Ernest Hemingway novel
53 Spinning-wheel product
54 Papal vestment
55 "No way, Sergei!"
56 Ashtabula's lake
57 Adversary
58 Indigo plant
59 Bed support
60 Stands for
61 *Beetle Bailey* boob

DOWN

1 Kelly of talk TV
2 One of baby's firsts
3 *Laura* author Caspary
4 Waterloo fighter
5 Flea-market deal
6 Adult insect
7 ___-bodied
8 Tops used in gambling
9 Boudoir furniture pieces
10 Wild parsnip
11 City WNW of Tulsa
12 H.H. Munro's pen name
13 Between ports
21 Adds turf to
22 Cow-headed goddess
25 "Air Music" composer
26 A Muse
27 Grafting shoot
28 Playground sight
29 Cultured gem
30 Like *The X-Files*
31 Dorothy's Oz visit, e.g.
33 French restaurant
36 Library regular
37 David of *Bones*
39 American Beauty
40 "Book 'em ___!"
42 January birthstone
43 They have their reservations
45 Detective Pinkerton
46 "Yes" votes
47 Take a spill
48 Song from *La Tosca*
49 Volcanic rock
50 Sandberg of baseball
51 Israeli premier (1969–74)

★★★ Binairo®

Complete the grid with zeros and ones until there are 5 zeros and 6 ones in every row and every column. No more than two of the same number can be next to or under each other. Rows or columns with exactly the same content are not allowed. There is only one valid solution.

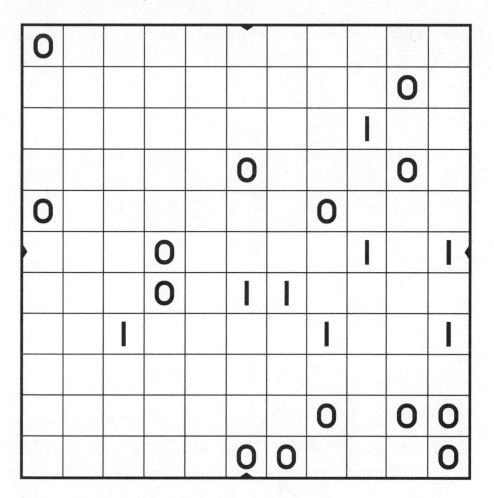

BLOCK ANAGRAM

Form the word that is described between parentheses with the letters above the grid. One or more extra letters are already in the right place.

GALOOTS (A study claiming divination by the positions of the planets and sun and moon)

★★★ Sudoku Twin

Fill in the grid so that each row, each column and each 3 x 3 frame contains
every number from 1 to 9. A sudoku twin is two connected 9 x 9 sudokus.

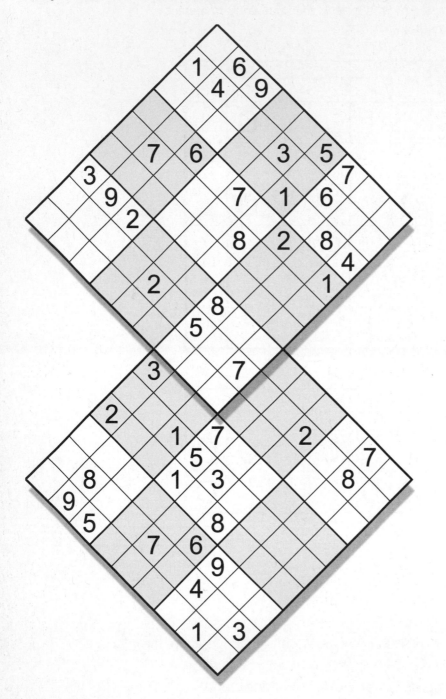

★★★ Sport Maze

Draw the shortest way from the golf ball to the hole. You can only move along vertical and horizontal lines, not along diagonal lines. The number on each square indicates the number of squares the ball must be moved in the same direction. You can change directions at each stop.

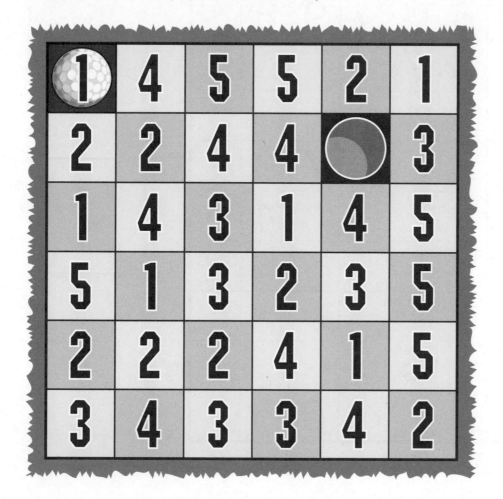

UNCANNY TURN

Rearrange the letters of this phrase to form a cognate anagram, one which is related or connected in meaning to the original. The answer can be one or more words.
ELEVEN PLUS TWO

★★★ Classic Sudoku

Fill in the grid so that each row, each column and each 3 x 3 frame contains every number from 1 to 9.

4			6			9	8	
		1	3	7				
	8		4	1				
	1					7	3	
							1	5
8	6							2
5								
	9	3		5				
						6		

DOODLER

A doodle puzzle is a combination of images, letters and numbers that stands for a word or concept. If you cannot solve a doodle puzzle, do not look at the answer right away. Try to solve it later or tomorrow. When you know the answer, study the puzzle to understand how it works. Explaining doodle puzzles to friends will also reinforce your comprehension.

★★★ Kakuro

Each number in a black area is the sum of the numbers that you have to fill in to the next empty boxes. The empty boxes that make up the sum are called a run. The sum of the across run is written above the diagonal in the black area, and the sum of the down run is written below the diagonal. Runs can only contain the numbers 1 through 9, and each number in a run can only be used once. The gray boxes only contain odd numbers and the white only contain even numbers.

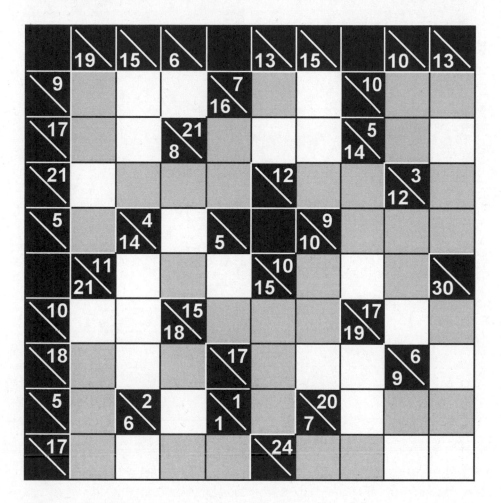

DELETE ONE

Delete one letter from one of these words and rearrange the rest to come up with a vocation.
RIM STY TIN

★★★ Parking Spaces

Which cars (1–6) belong in parking spaces A to G?

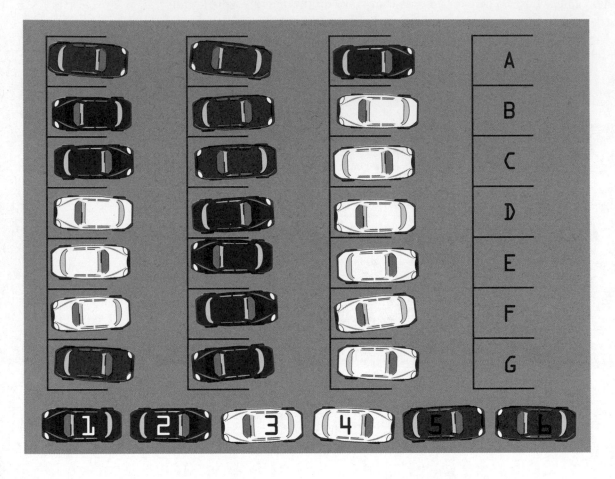

FIVES AND FOURS

Each line contains a five-letter and four-letter word that have been mixed together (the order of the letters in each word has not been changed). Unmix the two words on each line and write them in the spaces provided. When you're done, find a two-part answer to the clue by reading down the letter columns in the answers.

CLUE: Top of the bill?

```
SSPWOIRDT   — — — — — + — — — —
ZTAUBLLEU   — — — — — + — — — —
ASOABORVE   — — — — — + — — — —
MROADONAR   — — — — — + — — — —
```

★★★ Sudoku X

Fill in the grid so that each row, each column and each 3 x 3 frame contains every number from 1 to 9. The two main diagonals of the grid also contain every number from 1 to 9.

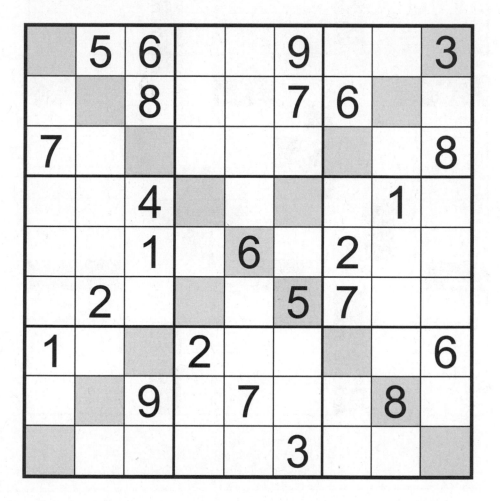

CHANGE ONE

Change one letter in each of these two words, to form a common two-word phrase.
  FOOD HATCH

★★★★ Show Tunes by Karen Peterson

ACROSS

1 *The King and I* heroine
5 Second prime minister of South Africa
10 Basics
14 ___ *Indigo*
15 "Luncheon on the Grass" painter
16 Take to the streets
17 Mr. Griffin
18 Ekberg in *La Dolce Vita*
19 Golfer Brett
20 Song from *Show Boat*
22 Eskers
23 "___ Day Goes By": Sondheim
24 Pack down
26 Some are floppy
29 Prank
32 Author LeShan
35 "Take ___" (A-Ha hit)
36 Swan lover of myth
37 San Francisco hill
38 *The Voyage* composer
40 Artist Ray
41 Mrs. Bob Dole
43 ___ de mer (seasickness)
44 Burnett of CNN
46 Ryan and Tilly
47 Piercing tool
48 Rover's rope
50 Fathers
51 Jake Black, at times
53 Mine approach
55 London statue
57 Song from *Can-Can*
63 Luke Skywalker's wife
64 Lloyd in *St. Louis Blues*
65 Barcelona bull
66 2008 Sean Penn film
67 Occurrence
68 Sharif in *Funny Girl*
69 Po tributary
70 "Le Foyer de la Danse" painter
71 *Take Me Or Leave Me* musical

DOWN

1 Bullets
2 Harrison or Coward
3 Van Brocklin of football
4 Breakthroughs
5 Like MENSA members
6 No. 1 song from *Flashdance*
7 Part of BYU
8 Mozambique city
9 Kicked off
10 ___ *With a View*: Forster
11 Song from *Sweet Charity*
12 Escalator clause
13 Suffix for young
21 Turndowns
25 Sea E of the Caspian
26 Church doctrine
27 Acquired relative
28 Song from *Gypsy*
30 Ladd and Lerner
31 Calligraphy tool
33 City to get out of
34 Chasm
39 Retail
40 Farrow in *September*
42 Copycat
45 Polite
49 Cigar city
50 Drink daintily
52 Honshu city
54 Fender flaws
55 Jane Austen novel
56 Icebox incursion
58 Heart's desire
59 Heavyweight Maskaev
60 The Spanish Steps site
61 Mideast land
62 Alphabetize

★★★★ Pixel Fun

Color the correct squares black and discover the pixel image. The numbers on the outer border against the black or the white background indicate the total number of black or white squares on a column or row. The numbers on the inner border indicate the largest group of adjacent black or white squares to be found anywhere on that column or row. For instance, if there is a six on the outer ring and a two on the inner ring against a white background, then there are six white blocks in that row, and the biggest group or groups consist of a maximum of two adjacent white blocks.

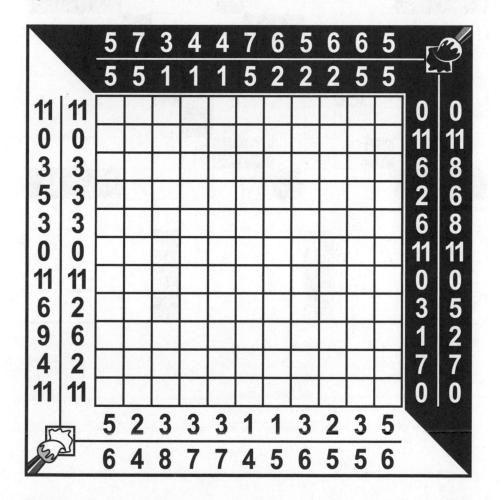

CHANGE THE NUMBER

Swap two numbers to make the figures add up to the correct sum.

```
  581
  254
 ____
  615
```

★★★★ Mr. Secretary by Karen Peterson

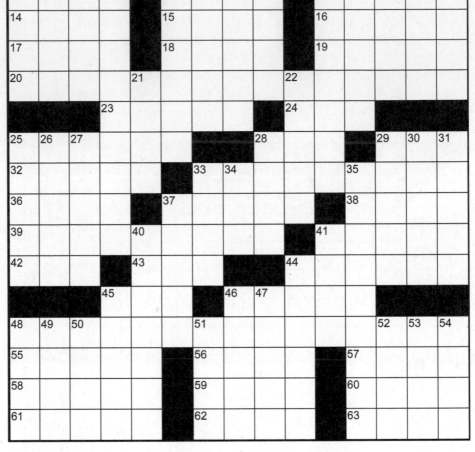

ACROSS

1 FDR's dog
5 *Hurlyburly* playwright
9 Snitch
14 Land of plenty?
15 Cross letters
16 Love to bits
17 Hexagram
18 Ten-speed option
19 Matt of *Today*
20 Secretary of the Treasury under Obama
23 Apt anagram for steno
24 PGA member
25 Rio dances
28 "My ___": Usher
29 Doo-wop's ___ Na Na
32 Break point
33 Johnson's 1964 opponent
36 133.322 pascals
37 Swings around
38 Crèche trio
39 What Mandela fought
41 Elaine of *Seinfeld*
42 ___ blu, dipinto di ...
43 Minute
44 Caress
45 "Fancy that!"
46 Endured
48 Secretary of the Treasury under Clinton
55 Torpedo firer
56 Lab gel
57 Charles Lamb alias
58 Tilting weapon
59 Least of the litter
60 1994 Jodie Foster film
61 Verbalize
62 Roy Orbison song
63 Fib

DOWN

1 Double-quick
2 Bubbly wine
3 Neeson in *Rob Roy*
4 Third vice president of the U.S.
5 Some turn signals
6 Keep ___ on (watch over)
7 Crows
8 Limerick locale
9 Gwyneth in *Emma*
10 Hells Canyon state
11 Sentence subject
12 Native Canadian
13 Title for Brahms
21 Flawlessly
22 Apple products
25 Darkness Prince
26 Ali's rope-___
27 Fable lesson
28 Extorted
29 Stephen King novel (with "The")
30 *The Science of Logic* author
31 Pop up
33 Euphoria
34 Michelle's assent
35 Bill of Rights member
37 Martin of *The West Wing*
40 Hi-fi speaker
41 Microphone type
44 Big day in July
45 Kelly in *High Noon*
46 Smooth transition
47 Blue Nile source
48 Humdinger
49 Like ___ out of hell
50 Practice
51 Carlson of *The Simpsons*
52 Parmenides' home
53 Creek
54 Clearance

★★★★ Binairo®

Complete the grid with zeros and ones until there are 6 zeros and 6 ones in every row and every column. No more than two of the same number can be next to or under each other. Rows or columns with exactly the same content are not allowed. There is only one valid solution.

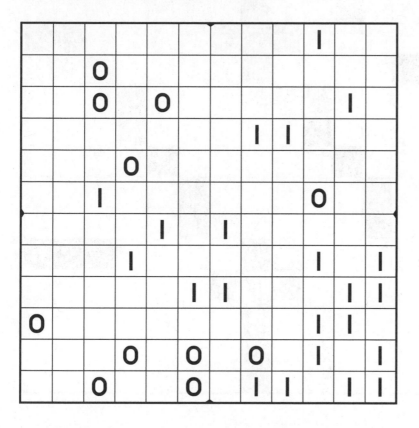

CHANGELINGS

Each of the three lines of letters below should spell the name of a city, but the letters have been mixed up. Four letters from the first name are now in the third line, four letters from the third name are in the second line and four letters from the second name are in the first line. The remaining letters are in their original places. What are the cities?

CASHINATOG
LOPENXRAEN
AWEHANDGNI

★★★★ Themeless by John McCarthy

ACROSS

1 *Marley & Me* actress
8 Luca in *Shark Tale*
15 Andrews Sisters member
16 Tia in *Wayne's World*
17 Oath
18 Doctored
19 Writer
20 Renaissance patron
21 Bonkers
23 Changed
26 *My Fair Lady* locale
29 Drive
31 251.9 calories
32 *A Confederacy of Dunces* author
33 Run out, in a sense
34 Spoon
35 Viking letter
36 Gives up
37 "He's not my ___"
38 American telecom co.
39 Line dance
40 Serbian tennis star
41 Debussy's "La ___"
42 Gastric woe
43 Hank of hair
44 Babble
46 Crystal-baller
48 Wax-glazed fabric
49 Noah's landfall
53 Kind of industry
56 "Marines' Hymn" city
57 Fashions
58 Jazzman Mose
59 Gloom
60 Adolescent

DOWN

1 *The Sound of Music* backdrop
2 One in on a bust
3 *Gosford Park* character Novello
4 Florida State athlete
5 Testimonial
6 Attack
7 Abigail Adams, ___ Smith
8 Columbus Day mo.
9 Haphazard
10 Railroad support
11 Be bombastic
12 *Young Frankenstein* star
13 Suffix for fail
14 Because, in Latin
22 It's golden, at times
23 Shows up
24 Daylong marches
25 Arm-twisting
26 *The Lady Is ___*
27 Alito colleague
28 Shrank
30 *Picnic* beauty queen
36 March Madness teams
37 Diamondback
39 Bargain-basement
40 Barren
45 Hyperion, for one
47 Baseball Hall-of-Famer Combs
50 "Horse Fair" painter Bonheur
51 Like a bump on ___
52 Antler branch
53 IV amounts
54 "... ___ mouse?"
55 Double curve
56 Sylvester, to Tweety

★★★★ Pixel Fun

Color the correct squares black and discover the pixel image. The numbers on the outer border against the black or the white background indicate the total number of black or white squares on a column or row. The numbers on the inner border indicate the largest group of adjacent black or white squares to be found anywhere on that column or row. For instance, if there is a six on the outer ring and a two on the inner ring against a white background, then there are six white blocks in that row, and the biggest group or groups consist of a maximum of two adjacent white blocks.

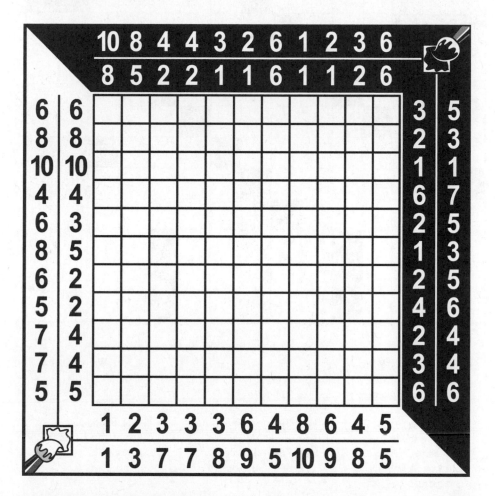

BLOCK ANAGRAM

Form the word that is described between parentheses with the letters above the grid. One or more extra letters are already in the right place.

CROATIAN (Foreseeing the future)

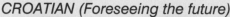

| | L | | | | V | | Y | | | |

★★★★ Lord Stanley's Cup by Don Law

ACROSS

1 Branch of math
5 Source of 25 Across
10 Landon and Neuman
14 *911* city
15 Utah mountains
16 Aggravate
17 Way off yonder
18 Casual goodbye
19 "___ Around": Beach Boys
20 2009 Stanley Cup winners
22 Island greetings
24 Appropriate
25 "___ of robins in her hair"
26 Harvest goddess
27 2008 Stanley Cup winners
30 Fuel-efficient Toyota
33 Add turf to
34 "Got you next time!"
35 Minus
36 Ex-Patriot Tony
37 "I'm better than you" sort
38 "Friendly Skies" airline: Abbr.
39 Leaking
40 Aries and Pisces
41 Flash Gordon and others
43 Terminus
44 Peter and a Wolfe
45 Mass sayers
49 Doc in *Cars*
51 1993 Stanley Cup winners
52 Minerals
53 Title for Macbeth
55 Scat singer Fitzgerald
56 Put on notice
57 Newspaper notices
58 Kid Rock hit
59 *The Sound of Music* baroness
60 Music for nine
61 In the cellar

DOWN

1 *The Sound of Music* family
2 Direct elsewhere
3 Puerile
4 Stunning
5 Spring blooms
6 Beaming
7 Arboreal Tolkien creatures
8 Sèvres summer
9 Susan in *Thelma & Louise*
10 Melodic pieces
11 2004 Stanley Cup winners
12 Red Hot Chili Peppers member
13 Volleyball stats
21 Camden Yards officials
23 Bawdy
25 "Belling the Cat" author
27 *Jurassic Park* bug trapper
28 "Please proceed"
29 B-team members
30 More than zero
31 Swing a sickle
32 1983 Stanley Cup winners
33 Steak orders
36 1988 Stanley Cup winners
37 Starry
39 Prefix for dynamic
40 Agitated condition
42 Sky King's plane
43 Borgnine in *Marty*
45 Venice's ___ di Rialto
46 Marge Simpson's sister
47 *Canterbury* ___
48 Viewpoint
49 NHL Hall-of-Famer Gordie
50 1,500 mile Russian chain
51 Street name
54 *Boardwalk Empire* network

★★★★ Binairo®

Complete the grid with zeros and ones until there are 5 zeros and 6 ones in every row and every column. No more than two of the same number can be next to or under each other. Rows or columns with exactly the same content are not allowed. There is only one valid solution.

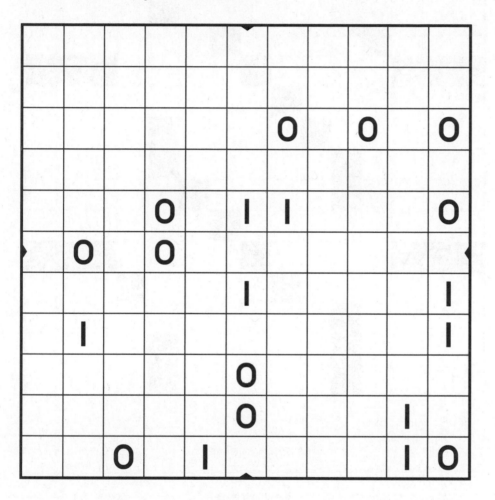

BLOCK ANAGRAM

Form the word that is described between parentheses with the letters above the grid. One or more extra letters are already in the right place.

ATHLETE (communication from one mind to another)

				P				**Y**

★★★★ The President's Men by John McCarthy

ACROSS

1 Internet language
5 Gelatinous garnish
10 Gen. ___ E. Lee
14 Richard in *Pollyanna*
15 Brazil seaport
16 Oriental servant
17 Attorney General under Obama
19 Prefix for graph
20 Tinker Bell's friend
21 "... ___ it just me?"
22 Faux gold
24 Hierarchy level
25 Peter Fonda title role
26 *Gomer Pyle, U.S.M.C.* star
29 Alvin or Simon
33 Short-horned antelope
34 Snub
35 Stick ___ in the water
36 Jawed tool
37 Bears may land here
38 "Drat!"
39 Ancient instrument
40 Sidle of *CSI*
41 Pervasive qualities
42 Bluegrass State
44 Teensy-___
45 Epoxy
46 Common barrier
47 Pirate Hands
50 Move, in realtor slang
51 "Kick it ___ notch": Emeril
54 Letter drop
55 Secretary of Education under Obama
58 Improve a road
59 Bug
60 "Put ___ on it!"
61 *Z* star Montand
62 Jed Clampett portrayer
63 SpongeBob's pet snail

DOWN

1 Nedry's *Jurassic Park* vehicle
2 Taj Mahal site
3 Vaunting
4 RSA political party
5 What squirrels squirrel away
6 Ninth baseball commissioner
7 Gridiron shoulder wear
8 Anger
9 Wozniacki of tennis
10 White House Chief of Staff under Obama
11 Melville book
12 *I Love Lucy* star
13 "How Great ___ Art"
18 Paradisiacal maiden
23 Salesperson
24 Secretary of Defense under Obama
25 *Star Trek* lieutenant
26 Kim in *Vertigo*
27 Greet the dawn
28 Range ruminant
29 Cautious
30 Traffic maneuver
31 ___ *a Stranger* (1955)
32 Nurse Ratched's creator
34 Fountain treat
37 Kiss
41 *Wheel of Fortune* buys
43 Suffix for glob
44 Thoreau's pond
46 Witherspoon in *Water for Elephants*
47 2002 Owen Wilson film
48 Belarussian, e.g.
49 Go a-wandering
50 Genetic strands
51 Where John Wooden coached
52 Low poker hand
53 Murray of tennis
56 Vicksburg soldier
57 Pick, pick, pick

★★★★ Pixel Fun

Color the correct squares black and discover the pixel image. The numbers on the outer border against the black or the white background indicate the total number of black or white squares on a column or row. The numbers on the inner border indicate the largest group of adjacent black or white squares to be found anywhere on that column or row. For instance, if there is a six on the outer ring and a two on the inner ring against a white background, then there are six white blocks in that row, and the biggest group or groups consist of a maximum of two adjacent white blocks.

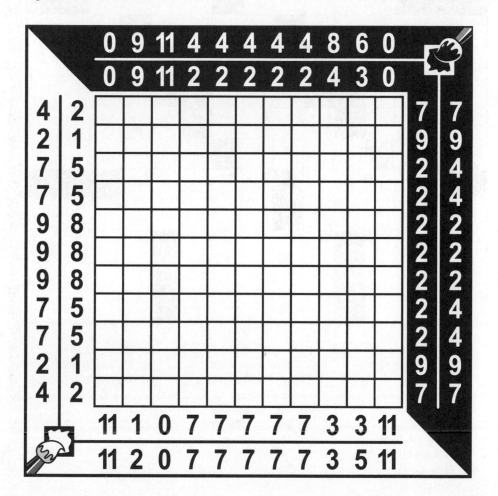

BACK TO FRONT

A palindrome is a word or phrase which reads the same from front to back and back to front, such as NUN, RADAR, MADAM and SOME MEN INTERPRET NINE MEMOS.
How many can you think of in 5 minutes?

★★★★ Celebrity Challenge by Michele Sayer

ACROSS

1 Adam's second son
5 Jesper Parnevik, for one
10 Fish swallowed by Monstro
14 Cager Bryant
15 Placates
16 Beatles film
17 *Law & Order: SVU* star
18 Be
19 Take the pressure off
20 2000 Cy Young Award winner
22 Deserved
24 "... not ___ mouse"
25 Self-centered
26 Some Buffalo wings
29 Killian's Irish Red, for one
31 Tachometer letters
34 Romantic couples
35 City on the Moselle
36 Kunis of *Family Guy*
37 Palin portrayer Fey
38 Oklahoma tribe
39 Gooding of *Deadwood*
40 "Measure of ___": Clay Aiken
41 German road
42 Rocker Reznor
43 Two-legged zebra
44 Ho Chi ___
45 Daisy Buchanan's admirer
46 Venom dispenser
48 Join forces
50 Boomtown Rats founder Bob
52 Elaine in *The Graduate*
56 Eagled a par-3 hole
57 Keys in the water
59 Enterprise navigator
60 Focal points
61 One monkey's "evil" words
62 Activist Brockovich
63 Sommer in *The Winds of War*
64 "Surprise" Symphony composer
65 Broadway beacon

DOWN

1 Tamiroff in *Lord Jim*
2 ___ Raton
3 Hairstylist José
4 Star seen late at night
5 Movie previews
6 Like candle drippings
7 Estée Lauder spokesmodel
8 *Dungeons & Dragons* arbiters: Abbr.
9 *Bobby* director Emilio
10 Oteri in *Scary Movie*
11 "We Can" singer
12 In addition
13 Gazette page
21 Big Daddy player Burl
23 Rhine tributary
26 Instrument in "Norwegian Wood"
27 Familiar "Turn, Turn, Turn" words
28 *State of Play* star
30 School on the Thames
32 Backup strategy
33 Doc Brown's friend
35 Eerie wind sound
36 *The Road* actor
41 2004 Tim Burton film
42 *Mon Oncle* director
44 L–P links
45 *The Beaver* star
47 Tatum's *Paper Moon* role
49 "Is there ___ to this madness?"
50 High wind
51 Green science: Abbr.
53 "You bet!"
54 Musical medley
55 Ex-senator Sam
58 Whole lot

★★★★ Binairo®

Complete the grid with zeros and ones until there are 6 zeros and 6 ones in every row and every column. No more than two of the same number can be next to or under each other. Rows or columns with exactly the same content are not allowed. There is only one valid solution.

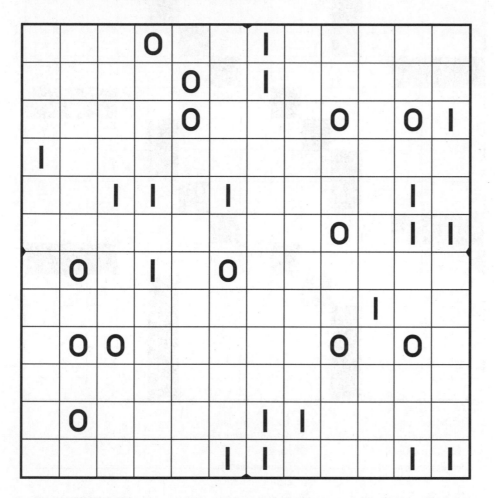

DOODLER

A doodle puzzle is a combination of images, letters and numbers that stands for a word or concept. If you cannot solve a doodle puzzle, do not look at the answer right away. Try to solve it later or tomorrow. When you know the answer, study the puzzle to understand how it works. Explaining doodle puzzles to friends will also reinforce your comprehension.

★★★★ Classic Co-stars by Michele Sayer

ACROSS

1 United ___ Emirates
5 Michaelmas daisy
10 Wide opening
14 Car for Trump
15 Après-ski
16 Glow
17 Couturier Cassini
18 Belmont bet
19 Coast Guard jail
20 Forearm bone
21 A pop
22 Hockey stick part
23 Rarin' to go
25 Antenna
26 Flatt of bluegrass
29 Izod Center, for one
31 Quintessential
32 Pesky insect
33 Nautilus captain
37 Legal claim
38 Dislodge
39 Teen sleuth Nancy
40 Look after
41 1975 Wimbledon winner
42 *Same Time, Next Year* dramatist
43 Juice the goose
45 Unlace
46 Wine bottle
49 Light refractor
51 November word
52 Help a thief
53 Morgiana's master
57 Lily Pons, e.g.
58 Dull
59 Olympian hawk
60 Daredevil Knievel
61 Carnival show
62 Russo in *The Thomas Crown Affair*
63 Inspiron computer
64 Ed heard in *Up*
65 Capt. Picard's friend

DOWN

1 Dominican baseball family
2 Lunar trench
3 Final word
4 *Key Largo* co-stars
5 Show up
6 Dieter's lunch
7 *Desk Set* co-stars
8 Emulate Dürer
9 "Comin' thro' the ___": Burns
10 *No Man of Her Own* co-stars
11 Acoustic
12 Vainglory
13 Rarin' to go
22 Affleck in *The Company Men*
24 Sushi fish
25 Regale
26 Buoyant song
27 Falco of *Nurse Jackie*
28 *Has Anybody ___ My Gal?*
30 Fulminate
32 Wind blast
34 Notable times
35 Ancient Persian
36 Wilson in *Midnight in Paris*
38 Diamond bag
42 *Lusitania*'s call
44 Astern
45 Highway eyesore
46 Gave up
47 "Stayin' ___"
48 Make merry
50 Zellweger in *Cinderella Man*
52 Word for Yorick
54 "Diamonds ___ girl's best ..."
55 Curved
56 Cruising
58 Victoria's Secret item

★★★★ Pixel Fun

Color the correct squares black and discover the pixel image. The numbers on the outer border against the black or the white background indicate the total number of black or white squares on a column or row. The numbers on the inner border indicate the largest group of adjacent black or white squares to be found anywhere on that column or row. For instance, if there is a six on the outer ring and a two on the inner ring against a white background, then there are six white blocks in that row, and the biggest group or groups consist of a maximum of two adjacent white blocks.

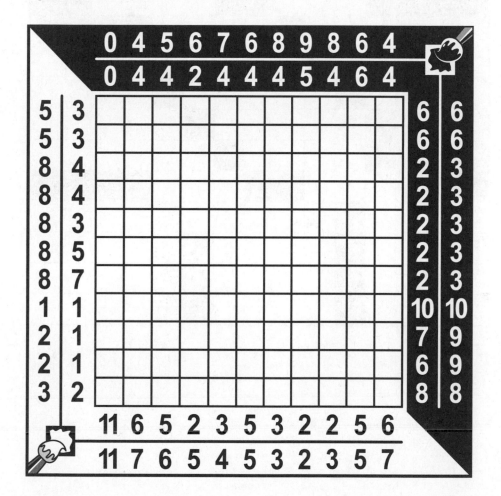

CROSS WORD?

This 11-letter word starts with the same letter it ends with. Add three of a kind, morning, army police, with two to find.

★★★★ Oil on Canvas by Michele Sayer

ACROSS

1 Winter Palace residents
6 Bay with gray
10 Jekyll's alter ego
14 Apportion
15 Further
16 "Be it ___ so humble ..."
17 Freetown coin
18 Lode
19 Flat fee
20 "Musicians in the Orchestra" painter
22 N. Carolina motto word
23 Saturn model
24 New York City river
26 Coax
30 Zesty flavor
32 *Hulk* director ___ Lee
35 Clean the slate
36 Minister's house
37 Neither go-with
38 Audition tape
39 Bar Harbor locale
40 Make eyes at
41 180° from WSW
42 The Donald's second
43 Sharp
44 Article in *Handelsblatt*
45 Rainbows
46 Piano type
47 Vortex
49 Gershwin or Newborn
50 Crazy bone
52 "Girl With a Pearl Earring" painter
59 Denver paper
60 District
61 Code name
62 A double reed
63 Palindromic hour
64 Related maternally
65 North, to Monet
66 Resort SE of Palermo
67 Fussed over

DOWN

1 Narrative
2 Iditarod Trail transport
3 Sleep like ___
4 *Oxford Blues* heroine
5 Mules are this
6 "Nevermore" quoter
7 Cassini of fashion
8 East of the Urals
9 "Baloney!"
10 Start of a toast
11 "Indefinite Divisibility" painter
12 TV rooms
13 Art Deco artist
21 Female rabbit
25 What Endymion never did
26 Surrendered
27 Game site
28 "The Rower" painter
29 Spanish bear
30 Tux
31 Grandma Moses
33 *U Turn* star
34 Garson in *Pride and Prejudice*
36 Painter Chagall
39 Peter Parker's love
40 Italian goose
42 Like a March hare
43 Startled
46 Eminent leader
48 Passé
49 The Donald's first
50 Versed in
51 Gray wolf
53 *East of Eden* character
54 Broadway luminary
55 Early hi-fi format
56 Part of QED
57 Renaissance patron
58 *The Third Man* director

★★★★ Binairo®

Complete the grid with zeros and ones until there are 5 zeros and 6 ones in every row and every column. No more than two of the same number can be next to or under each other. Rows or columns with exactly the same content are not allowed. There is only one valid solution.

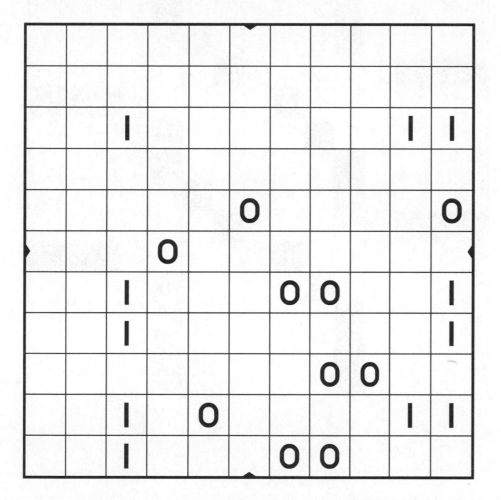

BLOCK ANAGRAM

Form the word that is described between parentheses with the letters above the grid. One or more extra letters are already in the right place.

TRACTOR (card used by fortunetellers)

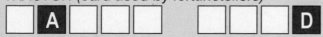

★★★★ Set in New York by Michele Sayer

ACROSS

1 1965 Beatles album
5 Leopard features
10 "A case of ___ die ..."
14 Wing-shaped
15 *I Pagliacci* clown
16 Fairytale heavy
17 Sitarist Shankar
18 Was Hamlet
19 Showy flower
20 Blueprint
21 Rhine tributary
22 *A Passage to India* heroine
23 Malediction
25 Muffle
26 Delightful
29 "What, me ___?": Neuman
31 Parlance
32 Miss Marple
33 *God's Little ___*: Caldwell
37 Feudal estate
38 Abominated
39 Envelope feature
40 Trial balloon
41 Burl in *The Big Country*
42 "All the world's a ___": Shak.
43 Cartoon Viking
45 Friend of Cowboy Curtis
46 Novelist Heller
49 Panache
51 Dictum
52 Suffix for bureau
53 ABBA's ballerina
57 "Spanish Eyes" assent
58 Succinct
59 Garlic quality
60 Bed board
61 2011 Johnny Depp film
62 Lena in *Chocolat*
63 Slippery
64 Dolin of ballet
65 *Quo Vadis* tyrant

DOWN

1 Symbol of Ireland
2 Tel Aviv carrier
3 Krakatoa outflow
4 Treat Williams film set in New York
5 Van Gogh's "The ___ Night"
6 *Hocus ___* (1993)
7 Marlon Brando film set in New York
8 Arena level
9 Instant lawn
10 Al Pacino film set in New York
11 Eyed greedily
12 Papal vestment
13 Fortification
22 ___ Lingus
24 Einstein's birthplace
25 Harriet Beecher Stowe book
26 English elevator
27 Garfield's friend
28 Gets in the game
30 Small bills
32 Cup of joe
34 Pincer
35 Seethe
36 Sword with a bell
38 Mighty partner
42 Small whale
44 Likely
45 George C. Scott film
46 James or Ventura
47 Black swan in *Black Swan*
48 Cordage fiber
50 *Thunderball* villain
52 Jackie heard in *Kung Fu Panda*
54 Like some rumors
55 Film ___
56 *New Yorker* cartoonist
58 Madrid Mrs.

★★★★ Pixel Fun

Color the correct squares black and discover the pixel image. The numbers on the outer border against the black or the white background indicate the total number of black or white squares on a column or row. The numbers on the inner border indicate the largest group of adjacent black or white squares to be found anywhere on that column or row. For instance, if there is a six on the outer ring and a two on the inner ring against a white background, then there are six white blocks in that row, and the biggest group or groups consist of a maximum of two adjacent white blocks.

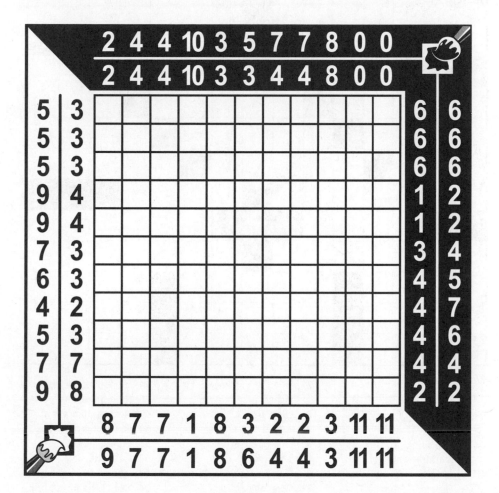

CHUCKLER

It starts with the same letter that it ends with, and there are two more of the same along the way, a pair of another, one each of two others, just to make you smile. What is the word?

★★★★★ Winning Spelling Bee Words

by John McCarthy

ACROSS

1 No-___ mutual fund
5 Common name of Alpha Cygnus
10 Noncoms
14 Scopes Trial org.
15 Tomato swelling
16 Senior lobby
17 Twist in a bar
18 Improv joke
19 5 Across is one
20 In an impertinent way
22 Chianti locale
24 Lock, stock and barrel
25 Fling to the mat
26 Planet visited by Flash Gordon
28 Winning word of 1940
31 "And now ..." sayer
34 ___ Romano (2001)
36 Victoria Island discoverer
37 Mr. Incredible Bob
38 Michigan Free Fair city
39 Cuban cow
40 Letters From ___ Jima (2006)
41 Join the club
42 "Old MacDonald" sounds
43 Green apple
45 Airbag, of a sort
47 Bluebird treat
48 Party punch?
52 Beatles' manager Brian
55 Changeling
56 1980s pesticide
57 Ghana's largest city
59 Spare item
60 Big fish
61 Rabbit fur
62 Gull kin
63 Noncoms
64 Bar of sorts
65 Gulf of Aqaba city

DOWN

1 Memory gap
2 View from Coney Island
3 Aboriginal Alaskan
4 Winning word of 1949
5 Cleveland Plain ___"
6 Whirlpool
7 ___ blu dipinto di blu
8 Beam
9 Headscarf
10 NEXTEL Cup org.
11 Winning word of 1959
12 Algerian seaport
13 Chipper
21 "Dies ___" (funeral hymn)
23 Loom part
27 Jeer at
28 Sing like a bird
29 52 cards
30 "For" votes
31 Sweeping story
32 Bryn ___
33 Winning word of 1970
35 "No, No, No" singer
38 Winning word of 1941
39 Winning word of 1952
41 "En garde" weapon
42 "Step ___!"
44 Hindu precepts
46 High ground
49 Mexican film award
50 Earth, in sci-fi films
51 "You ___ serious!"
52 Café sign
53 Free ad
54 "March Madness" org.
55 Domingo solo
58 Radar's rank: Abbr.

★★★★★ Binairo®

Complete the grid with zeros and ones until there are 5 zeros and 6 ones in every row and every column. No more than two of the same number can be next to or under each other. Rows or columns with exactly the same content are not allowed. There is only one valid solution.

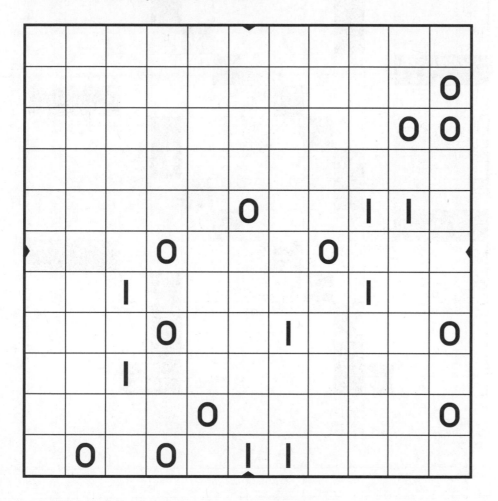

UNCANNY TURN

Rearrange the letters of this word to form a cognate anagram, one which is related or connected in meaning to the original. The answer can be one or more words.
  DORMITORY

★★★★★ Dancing with Fred by Michele Sayer

ACROSS

1 Harry Potter's Hedwig
4 Woodard in *Mandela*
9 Lobster trap
12 Competed
14 Sniggled
15 Compos mentis
16 Ballerina Pavlova
17 "The Highwayman" poet
18 Steamed
19 Pewter component
20 Oklahoma city
21 Beseech
22 Empty
24 Probable
25 City SE of Paris
28 Smiles
30 Hunter in *Crash*
31 Fall guy
32 Going into overtime
36 Notion: Comb. form
37 "Operator" singer Jim
38 Jim Davis dog
39 Broadway sign
40 Inventor Elias
41 Scrat's *Ice Age* quest
42 Scott in *Secretariat*
44 Big name in sunglasses
45 *Barbary Shore* author
48 Country singer Clark
50 Messed up
51 Bewail
52 Convent members
56 Dancing shoe
57 Twain's "Ah Sin" collaborator
58 Biting fly
59 Scams
60 Wicker wood
61 Corn Belt tower
62 Sancho's mount
63 Mountebank
64 *This Is Spinal ___* (1984)

DOWN

1 Ford's logo
2 Coq au vin ingredient
3 *Victory* heroine
4 Trojan War hero
5 Téa in *Spanglish*
6 Where Fred first danced with Ginger
7 Panpipe
8 Asner and O'Neill
9 "After they've seen ___ ..."
10 Shaq of the NBA
11 Nursery bear
13 Where Fred danced with Leslie
15 Where Fred danced with Cyd
21 Flagstick
23 Marina del ___
24 Vitamin-C source
25 Bony
26 Was a passenger
27 Stick in the fridge
29 Hare loss
31 Ralston of *127 Hours*
33 Pedestal figure
34 Hibernia
35 Disavow
37 *Burlesque* star
41 Bern river
43 Headed up
44 Cantankerous
45 Gene Pitney hit
46 Guthry and Eisenberg
47 Callaway clubs
49 Polished off
51 Pulpy mixture
53 Module
54 Lion King's queen
55 Give it a rest
57 Hip partner

★★★★★ Binairo®

Complete the grid with zeros and ones until there are 5 zeros and 6 ones in every row and every column. No more than two of the same number can be next to or under each other. Rows or columns with exactly the same content are not allowed. There is only one valid solution.

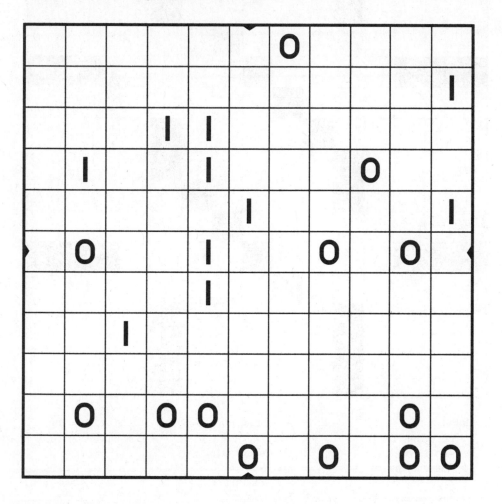

FIRST THINGS FIRST

Identify the phrase of a common final farewell from the first letters in each of its words.
W. W. N. F. Y.

★★★★★ Eclectic Mix by Michele Sayer

ACROSS

1 Sink or swim, e.g.
5 Hennessy and Ireland
10 A hole in the wall?
14 "En garde" weapon
15 "Arrivederci!"
16 Nuncupative
17 Ocean motion
18 Athletic competitions
19 A faux fur
20 Edinburgh daily, with "The"
22 1/3 a James Brown hit
24 "Follow me, Fido"
25 Visionary
26 Honda model
29 Minacious
33 Dry Italian wine
34 Big bins
35 Place for an icicle
36 Sheet of stamps
37 Sexy Beatles girl
38 Fairway obstacle
39 Mouse target
40 Richard in *Pollyanna*
41 Change a bill
42 "___ Trees in Flower": van Gogh
44 Like 76 trombones?
45 Amazon.com, for one
46 Diner's card
47 Clue in
50 Diana Ross film
54 Bamboozle
55 Watts in *The International*
57 Boxer Oscar De La ___
58 Once, formerly
59 Neckwear item
60 "___ Day Has Come": Celine Dion
61 Bit of folklore
62 Abated
63 Citi Field team

DOWN

1 Cat scanners?
2 *Aeneid*, for one
3 Alter the appearance of
4 Pastoral Symphony
5 Filled to capacity
6 "In an ___ world ..."
7 Creditor's claim
8 Nadal's reserve?
9 Hitchcock specialty
10 *Of Human Bondage* author
11 *The Magic Flute* solo
12 Groupies
13 *A Shot in the Dark* actress Sommer
21 All dried up
23 Aloha Day wear
25 1960s protest
26 Base for food glazes
27 Athletic advisor
28 Tippy craft
29 President of Egypt (1970–81)
30 Weight deductions
31 Smoothes out
32 Bassoon-like
34 Amorphous
37 Send up the river
41 Florentine river
43 "My country, ___ ..."
44 After
46 "Crazy Blues" singer Smith
47 "Beg pardon"
48 Blue fish in *Finding Nemo*
49 All-encompassing
50 Extinct ostrich cousins
51 Primo
52 "No way, Sergei!"
53 Course deviations
56 Epiphanic cry

PAGE 15

Optical Illusions

TRANSADDITION
TRANSPARENT

PAGE 16

Binairo®

I	O	I	O	O	I	O	O	I	O	I	I
O	I	O	I	I	O	O	I	I	O	O	I
I	I	O	I	O	O	I	I	O	I	O	O
I	O	I	O	O	I	I	O	I	O	I	O
O	O	I	O	I	I	O	O	I	I	O	I
I	I	O	I	O	I	I	O	O	I	O	O
O	O	I	O	I	I	O	I	O	I	O	I
O	I	O	I	I	O	I	O	I	O	I	O
I	O	I	I	O	O	I	O	O	I	I	O
O	I	O	O	I	I	O	I	O	I	O	I
I	O	I	I	O	I	O	O	I	O	I	O
O	I	O	O	I	O	I	I	O	I	O	I

CHANGELINGS
Longfellow, Wordsworth, Fitzgerald

PAGE 17

Familiar Address

P	A	E	R		S	K	A	T	E		D	I	E	T
E	C	R	U		T	A	L	E	S		E	T	T	E
R	E	S	T		A	B	O	R	T		F	E	T	E
M	R	T	A	M	B	O	U	R	I	N	E	M	A	N
			B	U	L	B		I	M	I	N			
T	A	M	A	L	E		S	T	A	N	D	A	R	D
E	T	A	G	E		B	I	O	T	A		T	O	R
N	A	N	A		C	A	D	R	E		D	O	G	E
A	R	I		B	E	L	L	Y		G	E	N	E	S
M	I	C	H	E	L	L	E		A	L	T	E	R	S
			E	R	L	E		C	L	E	A			
M	R	S	A	T	U	R	D	A	Y	N	I	G	H	T
I	B	A	R		L	I	A	R	S		L	E	A	H
L	I	N	T		A	N	D	E	S		E	R	T	E
A	S	K	S		R	A	S	T	A		D	E	E	M

PAGE 18

Madonna

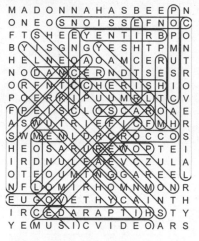

UNCANNY TURN
THAT QUEER SHAKE

PAGE 19

Cage the Animals

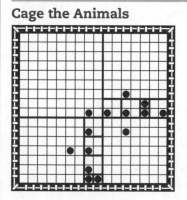

DOUBLE JUMBLES
Orange and Pomegranate
Chamois and Lizard
Parrot and Trout
Violet and Onion

PAGE 20

Kakuro

CORE PROBLEM
Initially they each sold apples at the rate of 3 for a dollar. No 1 sold ten dollars worth, No 2 eight dollars worth and No 3 seven dollars worth. No 1 had 3 apples left, No 2 had 5 and No 3 had 6. These then sold at one dollar each so their takings for the day were:

No 1: 10 + 3
No 2: 8 + 5
No 3: 7 + 6

PAGE 21

Cheese Escape

Three cheese cubes in the lower right corner.

LETTER BLOCKS
TEACHER
DENTIST

PAGE 22

Director's Chair

PAGE 23

Detectives

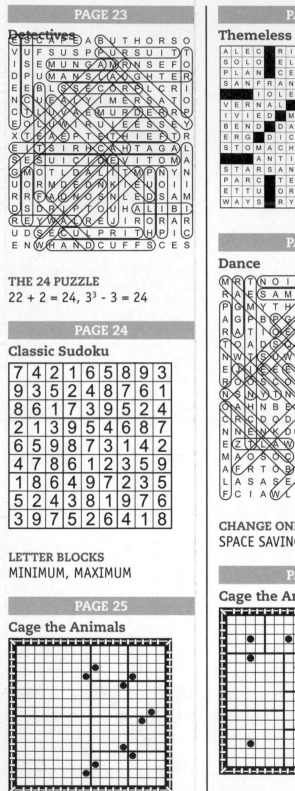

THE 24 PUZZLE
22 + 2 = 24, 3^3 - 3 = 24

PAGE 24

Classic Sudoku

7	4	2	1	6	5	8	9	3
9	3	5	2	4	8	7	6	1
8	6	1	7	3	9	5	2	4
2	1	3	9	5	4	6	8	7
6	5	9	8	7	3	1	4	2
4	7	8	6	1	2	3	5	9
1	8	6	4	9	7	2	3	5
5	2	4	3	8	1	9	7	6
3	9	7	5	2	6	4	1	8

LETTER BLOCKS
MINIMUM, MAXIMUM

PAGE 25

Cage the Animals

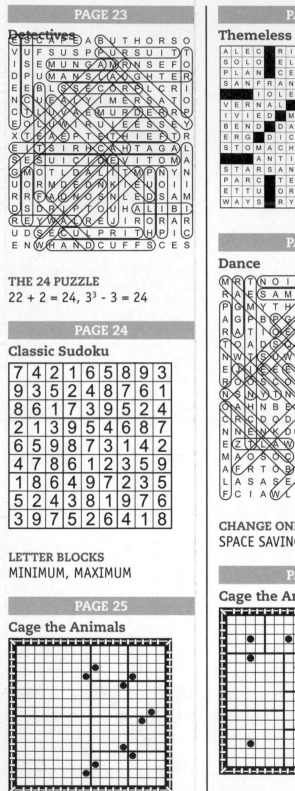

DELETE ONE
REBATE

PAGE 26

Themeless

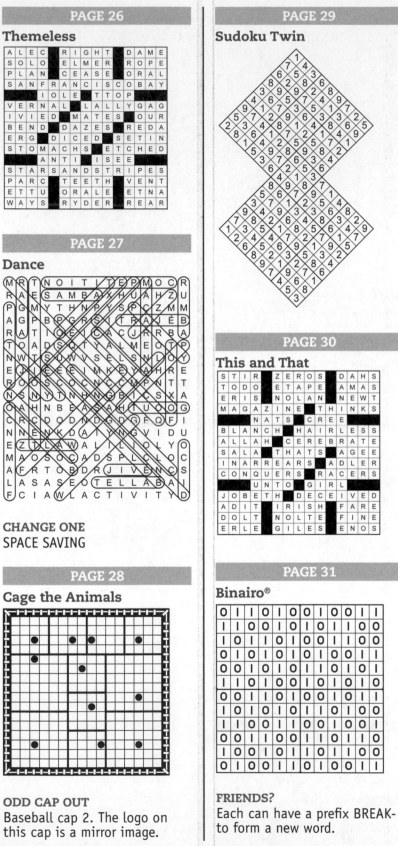

PAGE 27

Dance

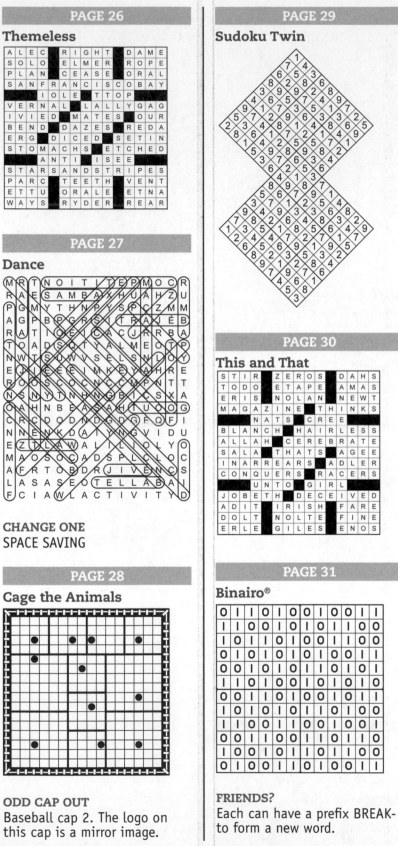

CHANGE ONE
SPACE SAVING

PAGE 28

Cage the Animals

ODD CAP OUT
Baseball cap 2. The logo on this cap is a mirror image.

PAGE 29

Sudoku Twin

PAGE 30

This and That

PAGE 31

Binairo®

0	1	1	0	1	0	0	1	0	0	1	1
1	1	0	0	1	0	1	0	1	1	0	0
1	0	1	1	0	1	0	0	1	1	0	0
0	1	0	1	0	1	0	1	0	0	1	1
0	0	1	0	1	0	1	1	0	1	0	1
1	1	0	0	1	0	0	1	0	1	0	1
0	0	1	1	0	1	0	0	1	1	0	0
1	0	1	0	1	1	0	0	1	0	1	0
1	1	0	0	1	0	1	1	0	0	1	0
0	0	1	1	0	1	0	0	1	0	1	0
1	0	1	0	1	1	0	1	1	0	0	1
0	1	0	0	1	1	0	1	0	0	1	1

FRIENDS?
Each can have a prefix BREAK- to form a new word.

PAGE 32

A Good Impression

Stamp B. The square in the top right-hand corner has been rotated 45°.

FIRST THINGS FIRST
Let sleeping dogs lie.

PAGE 33

Weather Forecast

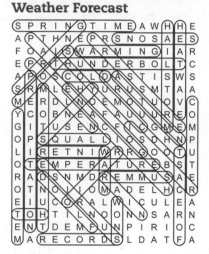

DOUBLETALK
mind

PAGE 34

Shady Puzzler

Color 2. The parasol is divided into 3 strips. The middle strip has the same color order as the two adjacent strips. If you start at color 2 this is the color order: 23614578.

SPOT THE DIFFERENCES

PAGE 35

Legends of the Game

PAGE 36

School

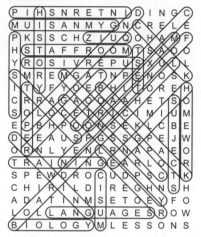

ANAGRAM
CODES   ENIGMAS

PAGE 37

Cage the Animals

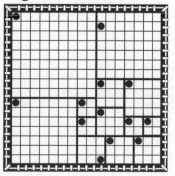

LETTER BLOCKS
BROTHER, HUSBAND

PAGE 38

Comedy Teams

PAGE 39

Classic Sudoku

7	4	5	6	1	8	2	3	9
2	8	3	7	9	5	6	4	1
6	9	1	4	2	3	5	8	7
1	2	9	8	7	6	3	5	4
5	7	4	9	3	2	1	6	8
3	6	8	5	4	1	7	9	2
8	5	2	1	6	9	4	7	3
9	3	7	2	5	4	8	1	6
4	1	6	3	8	7	9	2	5

FIVES AND FOURS
DREAMCAST
OLIVEGURU
WHITEBEAR
NAKEDBORN

PAGE 40

Word Sudoku

R	W	L	E	C	H	I	B	A
B	E	I	A	L	R	W	H	C
H	C	A	I	B	W	E	R	L
A	L	E	C	R	B	H	I	W
I	R	W	L	H	E	C	A	B
C	B	H	W	I	A	L	E	R
E	I	C	R	A	L	B	W	H
W	H	R	B	E	C	A	L	I
L	A	B	H	W	I	R	C	E

LETTER BLOCKS
SKIMMER, BLENDER

PAGE 41

Cubist Problem

Cube 2. The question mark can never be next to letter E.

SPOT THE DIFFERENCES

PAGE 42

Furniture

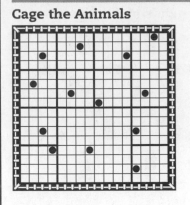

IS IT RIGHT?

A) irrideemable (should be irredeemable)

PAGE 43

Cage the Animals

CHANGELINGS
PANTOMIME, BURLESQUE, MELODRAMA

PAGE 44

Binairo®

0	1	0	1	0	1	1	0	0	1	1
1	0	1	1	0	1	0	0	1	0	1
0	1	1	0	1	0	1	1	0	1	0
1	0	0	1	1	0	0	1	0	1	1
1	1	0	1	0	1	0	0	1	0	1
0	1	1	0	1	0	1	0	1	1	0
1	0	1	0	1	0	1	0	1	0	0
0	1	0	1	0	1	0	1	1	0	1
0	0	1	1	0	1	1	0	1	1	0
1	0	1	0	1	0	1	1	0	1	0
1	1	0	0	1	1	0	1	1	0	0

HOW MUCH?
Jones had 48 and Smith had 30.

PAGE 45

Water Conservation

With showerhead 3, you only have 6 complete (12 half) holes instead of 9.

MISSING LETTER PROVERB
Waste not, want not.

PAGE 46

Divas

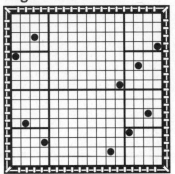

PAGE 47

Cage the Animals

WORDS IN HIDING
THRUSH, LOBSTER, STARLING, DEER, TENCH, HORSE

PAGE 48

Gray Scale Extremes

PAGE 49

Motorcycle

UNCANNY TURN
BAD CREDIT

PAGE 50

Binairo®

0	1	1	0	0	1	1	0	1	0	0	1
1	1	0	0	1	0	1	0	1	0	0	1
1	0	0	1	1	0	0	1	0	1	1	0
0	1	1	0	0	1	1	0	0	1	1	0
0	0	1	1	0	1	1	0	1	0	0	1
1	1	0	1	1	0	0	1	0	1	0	0
0	0	1	0	1	1	0	1	0	1	1	0
1	0	1	1	0	0	1	0	1	0	0	1
0	1	0	0	1	0	0	1	1	0	1	1
1	1	0	0	1	0	1	1	0	0	1	0
1	0	1	0	1	0	0	1	0	1	0	1

MISH-MATCH
ORANGE
CROCUS

PAGE 51

Kakuro

1	9	8		1	7	5
	8	5		6	8	
8	2	9	5		3	4
5			1	2	9	
		5	3	9		
8	4	1		6	1	2
9	3			8	4	

ALL IN A MUDDLE
TOMTIT
WEASEL

PAGE 52

Seeing Red

Tower 5.

SPOT THE DIFFERENCES

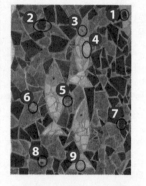

PAGE 53

Cage the Animals

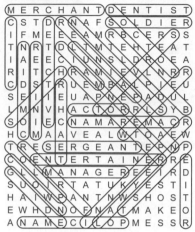

A CORNY QUESTION
A and B must get 2 full sacks,
and 2 empty and 3 half-full
and C gets 3 full, 3 empty and
1 half-full.
Or
A and B each take 3 full sacks,
3 empty sacks and 1 half-full,
and C takes 1 full, 1 empty and
5 half-full sacks.

PAGE 54

Professions

DELETE ONE
MARRIED

PAGE 55

Classic Sudoku

2	3	7	8	9	1	6	5	4
8	5	1	7	6	4	9	3	2
4	9	6	5	2	3	8	1	7
3	7	5	2	1	9	4	8	6
6	1	4	3	8	7	2	9	5
9	2	8	4	5	6	1	7	3
1	8	3	6	4	5	7	2	9
5	6	2	9	7	8	3	4	1
7	4	9	1	3	2	5	6	8

CHANGE ONE
SPRAY ON

PAGE 56

Letter Lining

abc in the word abcing. Every
group of three consecutive
letters in the text is
underlined.

LETTER BLOCKS
SWIMMING, BASEBALL

PAGE 57

Traffic Light

B	U	S	H		B	U	R	S	T		L	I	E	U
A	N	T	E		U	T	I	L	E		E	R	A	T
R	I	L	L		T	A	T	A	R		S	A	V	E
S	T	O	P	S	T	H	E	P	R	E	S	S	E	S
		L	O	O	N			A	T	E				
A	S	T	E	R	N		E	S	P	R	E	S	S	O
T	H	O	S	E		A	N	N	I	E		N	P	R
T	A	T	S		C	L	E	A	N		M	O	U	E
I	D	A		B	L	I	M	P		K	A	R	M	A
C	E	L	E	R	I	T	Y		U	N	I	T	E	D
		L	I	P		O	P	E	N					
G	O	J	U	M	P	I	N	T	H	E	L	A	K	E
A	V	I	D		E	R	A	T	O		A	R	I	A
B	A	B	E		R	A	V	E	L		N	E	W	T
S	L	E	D		S	N	E	R	D		D	A	I	S

PAGE 58

Cage the Animals

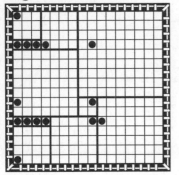

REVERSALS
Spin–nips, Tang–gnat, Deed–deed

PAGE 59

Sukodu Twin

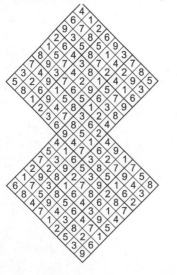

PAGE 60

Athletics

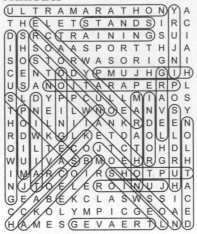

IN HARMONY
They can be played on a musical instrument.

PAGE 61

Word Sudoku

H	A	R	N	W	J	Z	O	I
I	O	J	Z	A	R	H	N	W
Z	W	N	I	O	H	J	A	R
W	J	A	O	H	N	I	R	Z
O	H	Z	J	R	I	A	W	N
N	R	I	W	Z	A	O	J	H
A	I	W	H	N	O	R	Z	J
R	N	H	A	J	Z	W	I	O
J	Z	O	R	I	W	N	H	A

THE NUMBER IS THE QUESTION
20. Egg white = 10. Yolk = +1. Yolk outside the egg white = -1.

PAGE 62

Sudoku X

9	6	5	4	7	2	1	3	8
3	1	4	9	8	6	5	7	2
8	2	7	5	3	1	6	9	4
1	8	6	2	9	4	7	5	3
4	9	3	8	5	7	2	6	1
5	7	2	1	6	3	4	8	9
6	4	9	3	1	5	8	2	7
7	3	1	6	2	8	9	4	5
2	5	8	7	4	9	3	1	6

TRANSADDITION
CONSTITUTION

PAGE 63

Binairo®

0	0	1	1	0	0	1	0	1	1	0	1
1	0	0	1	0	1	0	1	1	0	1	0
0	1	1	0	1	0	0	1	0	1	0	1
0	1	0	0	1	0	1	0	1	0	1	1
1	0	1	1	0	1	0	0	1	1	0	0
0	0	1	0	1	0	1	1	0	0	1	1
0	1	0	1	0	1	0	1	0	1	0	1
1	0	1	0	1	0	1	0	1	0	1	0
1	0	1	0	0	1	0	0	1	1	0	0
0	0	1	0	1	1	0	1	0	0	1	1
1	1	0	0	1	1	0	1	0	0	1	0
1	1	0	1	1	0	1	0	0	1	0	0

SUMMING UP
MISFORTUNE
1234567890

PAGE 64

Classic Sudoku

1	8	6	5	2	4	7	3	9
7	5	2	9	3	6	8	1	4
9	4	3	1	8	7	5	6	2
5	9	7	2	4	1	3	8	6
6	1	8	3	5	9	2	4	7
3	2	4	6	7	8	9	5	1
2	7	5	4	6	3	1	9	8
8	6	9	7	1	5	4	2	3
4	3	1	8	9	2	6	7	5

DOUBLETALK
plug

PAGE 65

Number Cluster

IDIOMATICALLY SPEAKING
Hoist with one's own petard.

PAGE 66

Keep Going

DIARY NOTE
All of them.

PAGE 67

Binairo®

0	0	1	1	0	1	1	0	1	0	1
1	0	0	1	1	0	0	1	1	0	1
0	1	1	0	1	1	0	1	0	1	0
1	1	0	1	0	0	1	0	1	1	0
1	0	1	1	0	1	0	0	1	0	1
0	1	1	0	1	0	1	1	0	0	1
1	1	0	0	1	1	0	1	0	1	0
0	0	1	1	0	1	1	0	1	1	0
1	1	0	0	1	0	1	0	1	0	1
0	0	1	0	1	1	0	1	0	1	1
1	1	0	1	0	0	1	1	0	1	0

SPEAKING VOLUMES
A bibliopole.

PAGE 68

Domino Effect

3 dots. The first group of dominoes forms the number 9 and contains a total of 9 spots. The second group forms the number 5, so it will contain 5 spots.

LETTER BLOCKS
TEMPLE, TONGUE

PAGE 69

Sudoku X

2	3	7	9	5	8	4	6	1
1	5	4	3	6	2	9	7	8
8	9	6	1	7	4	3	5	2
7	2	1	8	9	5	6	4	3
3	8	5	6	4	7	2	1	9
6	4	9	2	1	3	7	8	5
4	7	8	5	2	9	1	3	6
5	6	2	7	3	1	8	9	4
9	1	3	4	8	6	5	2	7

LONELY WORDS
Month, orange, silver, and purple.

PAGE 70

Reindeer Games

N	A	R	C		D	A	T	E	R		C	A	R	L
O	L	E	A		A	R	R	A	U		O	D	I	E
E	V	E	N		S	T	A	N	D		M	A	G	I
L	A	D	D		H	U	M		O	P	E	R	A	S
			Y	S	E	R		S	L	A	T			
D	A	N	C	E	R		V	I	P	S		J	E	B
O	C	E	A	N		K	I	T	H		N	O	M	E
G	R	A	N	T		L	X	I		M	O	D	E	L
M	E	T	E		P	E	E	N		O	R	I	E	L
A	S	H		E	R	I	N		D	O	T	E	R	S
			C	L	A	N		M	O	T	H			
A	U	T	U	M	N		T	E	N		P	A	T	S
S	T	O	P		C	O	H	A	N		O	M	I	T
T	E	R	I		E	N	U	R	E		L	A	R	A
A	P	E	D		R	A	D	A	R		E	D	E	R

PAGE 71

Number Cluster

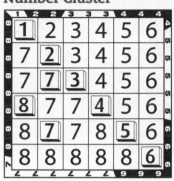

DOUBLETALK
Fast—The athlete runs fast. The wheel was stuck fast in the mud.

PAGE 72

Keep Going

GREEDY LETTER
W

PAGE 73

Holiday Viewing

H	E	A	T		R	A	J	A	H		D	E	O
A	R	C	H		E	M	I	L	E		W	I	N	D
L	I	R	E		L	I	N	E	R		H	A	T	E
L	E	E	S		E	G	G		S	P	I	N	E	T
			A	R	N	O	L	D		S	T	A	R	S
W	A	L	N	U	T		E	E	R	I	E			
A	L	A	T	E		G	A	R	N		C	L	E	O
N	A	S	A		M	E	L	B	A		H	A	R	D
D	I	S	C		O	N	L	Y		E	R	N	I	E
			L	I	M	I	T		B	R	I	A	N	S
B	L	E	A	T		C	H	E	E	R	S			
R	O	B	U	S	T		E	L	A		T	R	I	P
E	R	O	S		E	L	W	E	S		M	I	R	O
A	N	N	E		R	I	A	N	T		A	C	M	E
D	A	Y		M	A	Y	A	S		S	H	A	M

PAGE 74

Word Sudoku

C	A	W	I	F	N	T	O	H
N	H	F	O	T	A	I	C	W
T	O	I	H	C	W	N	F	A
F	I	A	N	H	C	W	T	O
O	W	T	F	A	I	H	N	C
H	N	C	W	O	T	A	I	F
I	C	N	A	W	F	O	H	T
A	T	H	C	N	O	F	W	I
W	F	O	T	I	H	C	A	N

SOUND ALIKE
beat/beet

PAGE 75

Time to Reflect

HIDDEN WORDS
IVANHOE, I-van-hoe

PAGE 76

Bring Me Sunshine

A4, A7, B2, C4, C6, E2, E5.

OOPS!
Bohemia had no coastline.

PAGE 77

Sudoku Twin

PAGE 78

Surf's Up

515253. Surfers on the same team have a number that forms an ascending series across all the sails. For example, the white team has the numbers 79-80-81, 82-83-84, 85-86-87.

FIVES AND FOURS

S T E A M H I S S
O P E R A C L A P
F R U I T L O G O
T O T E M T E N T

PAGE 79

Number Cluster

6	7	7	3	8	8
6	7	3	3	8	4
6	7	5	5	8	4
6	7	5	5	8	4
6	7	5	2	8	4
6	7	1	2	8	8

IN OTHER WORDS
Together (To-get-her)

PAGE 80

Keep Going

RUNNING REPAIRS
restores

PAGE 81

Binairo®

0	I	0	0	I	I	0	I	I	0	I	0
I	0	I	0	I	0	I	0	0	I	I	0
I	I	0	I	0	0	I	0	I	0	0	I
0	0	I	I	0	I	0	I	0	I	I	0
I	I	0	0	I	0	I	I	0	0	I	0
0	0	I	0	I	I	0	0	I	I	0	I
0	0	I	0	I	0	I	0	I	I	0	I
I	I	0	I	0	I	0	I	0	0	I	0
I	I	0	0	I	I	0	I	0	0	0	I
0	0	I	I	0	0	I	I	0	I	0	I
I	I	0	I	0	0	I	0	0	I	I	0
0	0	I	0	I	I	0	I	I	0	0	I

CHANGE ONE
Better grip

PAGE 82

Classic Sudoku

3	2	8	1	7	6	9	5	4
4	9	7	2	3	5	8	1	6
5	6	1	9	8	4	3	2	7
2	5	9	3	4	1	6	7	8
8	1	6	7	2	9	5	4	3
7	4	3	6	5	8	1	9	2
1	3	4	8	9	2	7	6	5
6	8	5	4	1	7	2	3	9
9	7	2	5	6	3	4	8	1

NOT IN ANY STATE
Q

PAGE 83

Kakuro

ALL ALONE
43 (all the others are greater than a square by 1)

PAGE 84

Early TV

PAGE 85

Wriggler

Worm B. Eyes: an eye from each worm. Color on the body: purple is dominant. The number of body sections: 5 is dominant over 4.

UNCANNY TURN
THE CLASSROOM

PAGE 86

Number Cluster

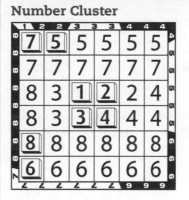

IMPORTANT CAPITAL
Polish

PAGE 87

Keep Going

WORD POWER
A "crash"

PAGE 88

In the Box

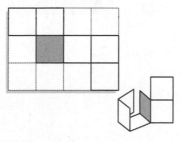

IN REVERSE
Reed/Deer

PAGE 89

Bring Me Sunshine

A3, A7, B5, C2, C7, E1, E5, E7.

LETTER BLOCKS
SIXTEEN, SEVENTY

PAGE 90

Number Cluster

DELETE TWO
CARTHORSE

PAGE 91

Keep Going

ECONOMICAL
Deeded

PAGE 92

Hair of the Dog

3 and 6. From drinks 1, 2, 4 and 5 you definitely will not get a hangover. That only leaves drinks 3 and 6.

AN APPLE A DAY
They need to be grandfather, father and son so the grandfather is a father and the middle father is both a father and a son.

PAGE 93

Binairo®

I	I	O	I	O	I	I	O	I	O	O
I	I	O	O	I	I	O	O	I	O	I
O	O	I	O	I	O	I	I	O	I	I
I	I	O	I	O	O	I	O	I	I	O
O	O	I	O	I	I	O	I	I	O	I
I	I	O	I	O	O	I	I	O	O	I
O	I	I	O	I	I	O	O	I	I	O
I	O	I	I	O	I	O	I	O	I	O
O	I	O	I	I	O	I	I	O	O	I
I	O	I	O	I	I	O	O	I	I	O
O	O	I	I	O	O	I	I	O	I	I

BLOCK ANAGRAM
ANABOLIC STEROID

PAGE 94

Number Cluster

WORKPLACES
SALESMEN, DIVER, MINISTER,
TEACHER, TRAINER

PAGE 95

Keep Going

MISSING LETTER PROVERBS
Penny wise, pound foolish.

PAGE 96

Inventions

PAGE 97

Double Dutch

PANJABEN. The letter groups
JA, PAN, B and EN have their
own symbol and are translated
from top to bottom.

FIRST THINGS FIRST
May the road rise up to meet
you.

PAGE 98

Kakuro

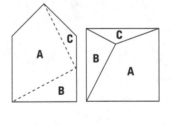

SHOWROOM SHUFFLE
40 cars

PAGE 99

Bond Girls

PAGE 100

Classic Sudoku

6	3	9	7	2	5	8	1	4
8	7	5	3	1	4	9	6	2
1	4	2	8	9	6	5	3	7
5	9	8	4	3	1	2	7	6
4	2	6	5	7	9	3	8	1
3	1	7	2	6	8	4	9	5
9	5	4	1	8	7	6	2	3
7	6	3	9	4	2	1	5	8
2	8	1	6	5	3	7	4	9

DON'T BE FLOORED!

PAGE 101

Spaced Out

Orbit C. The electrons in all the
other orbits respect the same
clockwise color sequence.

CHANGE ONE
stay put

PAGE 102

Word Sudoku

D	C	I	T	W	P	Q	E	V
V	E	Q	C	D	I	W	T	P
P	W	T	V	E	Q	D	C	I
W	D	C	E	Q	V	P	I	T
E	T	P	I	C	D	V	Q	W
Q	I	V	W	P	T	E	D	C
C	V	E	D	T	W	I	P	Q
T	Q	W	P	I	E	C	V	D
I	P	D	Q	V	C	T	W	E

SANDWICH
FRAME

PAGE 103

Number Cluster

FRIENDS?
Each can have the prefix
UNDER- to form a new word.

PAGE 104

Keep Going

FIRST THINGS FIRST
Time waits for no man.

PAGE 105

Sudoku Twin

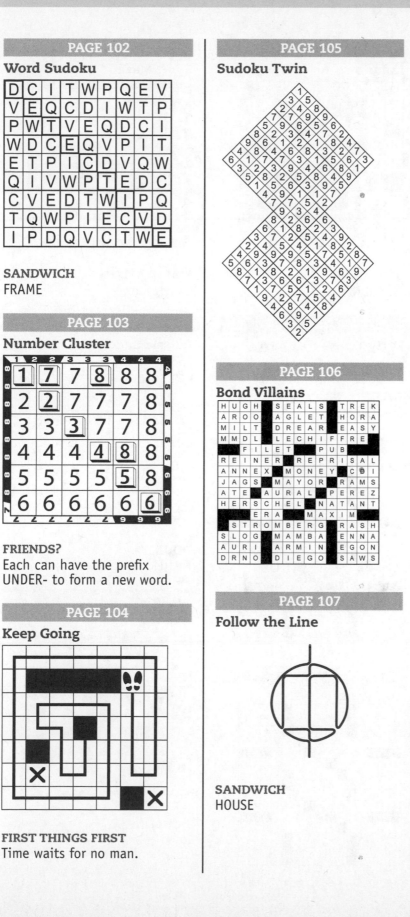

PAGE 106

Bond Villains

H	U	G	H		S	E	A	L	S		T	R	E	K
A	R	O	O		A	G	L	E	T		H	O	R	A
M	I	L	T		D	R	E	A	R		E	A	S	Y
M	M	D	L		L	E	C	H	I	F	F	R	E	
	F	I	L	E	T			P	U	B				
R	E	I	N	E	R		R	E	P	R	I	S	A	L
A	N	N	E	X		M	O	N	E	Y		C	D	I
J	A	G	S		M	A	Y	O	R		R	A	M	S
A	T	E		A	U	R	A	L		P	E	R	E	Z
H	E	R	S	C	H	E	L		N	A	T	A	N	T
	E	R	A			M	A	X	I	M				
	S	T	R	O	M	B	E	R	G		R	A	S	H
S	L	O	G		M	A	M	B	A		E	N	N	A
A	U	R	I		A	R	M	I	N		E	G	O	N
D	R	N	O		D	I	E	G	O		S	A	W	S

PAGE 107

Follow the Line

SANDWICH
HOUSE

PAGE 108

Number Cluster

4	4	2	7	7	7
4	4	2	8	7	7
8	8	8	8	7	7
8	3	1	6	6	6
8	3	3	6	6	6
8	5	5	5	5	5

BLOCK ANAGRAM
BETA BLOCKER

PAGE 109

Winner's Circle

H	U	G	H		C	A	L	E	B		M	O	L	D
A	C	R	E		A	N	O	L	E		O	L	A	Y
S	L	I	D		E	N	O	L	A		J	A	N	E
P	A	N	G		S	U	P	E	R	S	A	V	E	R
	D	E	C	A	L			C	I	V				
M	A	S	H	E	R		S	C	A	R	E	S	U	P
E	X	T	O	L		S	P	A	T	S		P	S	I
C	L	O	G		S	W	A	P	S		P	E	A	T
C	E	N		D	E	A	R	E		B	O	N	G	O
A	D	E	Q	U	A	T	E		G	A	R	D	E	N
		A	L	L			C	O	S	T	A			
S	U	N	N	Y	S	H	A	L	O		R	B	I	S
T	R	O	T		H	O	M	E	D		A	U	D	I
L	A	N	A		U	S	U	A	L		I	C	E	T
O	L	E	S		T	E	R	R	Y		T	K	O	S

PAGE 110

Stormy Weather

A2, A4, A7, C1, C4, C6, E3, E6.

TRANSADDITION
MAN OF DISTINCTION

PAGE 111

Kakuro

1	8	6		6	9	7		9
3		4	6	9	2		6	7
	8	2	4		5	7	9	6
3	9	7			8	9		4
2		1	5	3		8	4	5
4	6		8	1	4		6	
	1	7			1		1	3
1	3	9	4	2		1	2	
2	8		1	6		6	9	5

ANAGRAM
ARREST STOP BAR END

PAGE 112

Number Cluster

UNCANNY TURN
Cash lost in 'em

PAGE 113

Cubed

Piece 4. Only the pieces 2, 4 and 6 consist of the 10 blocks that you need to complete the cube. Only piece 4 has the right shape and the right colors.

INHERITANCE TEST

PAGE 114

Keep Going

DOUBLETALK
stick

PAGE 115

Kakuro

9	8	1	■	9	5	8	4
5	1	■	■	4	3	■	3	8
■	3	2	9	7	■	1	2	9
8	6	■	■	6	2	5	■	■
4	9	3	1	■	8	9	5
■	■	7	3	9	4	■	1	7
7	5	2	■	1	3	5	■	8
1	2	■	7	2	■	2	4	1
9	1	■	9	7	■	9	5	2

BLOCK ANAGRAM
HORMONES

PAGE 116

Party Time

Dice on 3.

DELETE ONE
SOLUTION

PAGE 117

Augusta Winners

P	E	T	S	■	M	O	T	E	T	■	S	T	E	P
U	N	I	O	■	U	R	I	A	H	■	E	R	D	A
L	O	G	Y	■	G	E	E	S	E	■	S	A	G	A
P	L	E	B	■	G	A	R	Y	P	L	A	Y	E	R
■	■	R	E	W	E	D	■	■	L	A	M	■	■	■
E	D	W	A	R	D	■	■	A	C	A	D	E	M	I	C
L	O	O	N	Y	■	B	E	L	I	E	■	A	W	E
M	O	O	S	■	B	O	R	O	N	■	A	R	I	D
E	N	D	■	C	R	A	I	G	■	A	N	K	L	E
R	E	S	O	L	U	T	E	■	A	R	N	O	L	D
■	■	R	A	S	■	■	O	D	I	U	M	■	■	■
V	I	J	A	Y	S	I	N	G	H	■	L	E	S	E
E	L	A	N	■	E	M	I	L	E	■	L	A	I	R
R	I	G	G	■	L	I	N	E	R	■	E	R	G	O
B	A	S	E	■	S	N	O	R	E	■	D	A	N	S

PAGE 118

Top-Ranked

R	S	V	P	■	B	A	C	O	N	■	G	U	L	L
I	T	E	R	■	E	T	A	P	E	■	E	S	A	U
G	I	G	I	■	T	E	P	I	D	■	N	E	W	T
G	R	A	V	I	T	A	T	E	■	V	E	R	S	E
■	■	A	R	O	M	A	■	■	P	A	R	■	■	■
C	A	S	T	O	R	■	I	D	I	T	A	R	O	D
A	R	L	E	N	■	I	N	R	E	■	L	I	L	I
P	E	E	P	■	L	A	K	E	R	■	H	A	L	S
O	N	E	R	■	E	G	A	D	■	S	O	N	I	C
N	A	P	O	L	E	O	N	■	B	A	S	T	E	S
■	■	P	I	S	■	G	R	A	S	P	■	■	■	■
B	L	E	E	P	■	P	A	U	L	S	I	M	O	N
R	E	A	R	■	P	U	R	S	E	■	T	I	R	E
E	A	S	T	■	A	R	O	S	E	■	A	C	E	R
T	H	E	Y	■	C	R	O	O	N	■	L	E	N	D

PAGE 119

Sport Maze

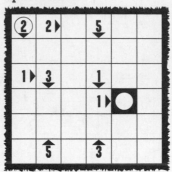

SOUND ALIKE
aloud/allowed

PAGE 120

Classic Sudoku

6	8	7	5	2	1	3	4	9
1	5	9	3	7	4	2	8	6
2	4	3	9	8	6	1	5	7
7	3	4	6	1	9	5	2	8
5	9	2	4	3	8	7	6	1
8	1	6	2	5	7	4	9	3
4	7	8	1	6	5	9	3	2
3	6	5	7	9	2	8	1	4
9	2	1	8	4	3	6	7	5

DOODLER
FatHER

PAGE 121

Kakuro

5	9	4	■	5	1	■	4	8
7	4	■	4	3	8	■	9	6
2	1	7	9	■	5	3	■	3
3	■	6	■	■	8	4	1	■
■	7	9	6	■	6	2	5	■
5	2	■	2	9	1	■	9	7
4	3	2	■	8	2	9	■	5
6	■	3	■	3	■	3	1	6
9	7	5	1	■	4	8	2	9

DOUBLETALK
hood

PAGE 122

Place Your Bets

Number 17. The value per token is as follows: A= 1, B= 5 and C= 10. The player places a token of equal value on the number.

IS IT RIGHT?

D) unprincipaled (should be unprincipled)

PAGE 123

The Wet Set

P	A	R	R			A	R	O	S	E			J	O	G
O	D	I	U	M		S	O	P	H	S			O	R	O
M	U	D	D	Y	W	A	T	E	R	S			A	A	R
P	E	S	E	T	A		E	R	E			A	N	T	E
		S	H	I	M		A	D	J	U	R	E	D		
S	U	B	T	O	T	A	L			S	A	R	I		
P	S	I		S	O	L	A	N			R	A	V	E	N
I	D	L	E		N	A	B	O	B			L	E	D	A
T	A	L	L	Y			Y	E	T	I	S			R	I	M
			Y	O	U	R		L	I	C	E	N	S	E	E
D	R	O	P	L	E	T		N	A	N	O				
R	A	C	E		P	O	I			R	O	B	R	O	Y
U	K	E		G	A	R	T	H	B	R	O	O	K	S	
B	E	A		A	S	T	H	E			A	D	D	L	E
S	S	N		S	T	E	E	P			Y	E	A	R	

PAGE 124

U.S. History

P	O	S	H		M	S	N	B	C		K	A	L	E
U	V	E	A		A	P	O	O	R		A	M	I	D
B	U	R	R		T	U	R	B	O		B	O	N	E
	M	A	R	T	I	N	V	A	N	B	U	R	E	N
			Y	A	N	K		K	A	L				
S	W	A	R	M	S		M	A	I	L		S	H	E
P	O	L	E	S		M	A	T	T	D	A	M	O	N
O	R	B	I		S	E	T	A	E		M	I	T	T
D	R	E	D	S	C	O	T	T		T	Y	L	E	R
E	Y	E		W	A	N	E		N	I	C	E	L	Y
			G	A	L			S	O	D	A			
F	R	A	N	K	L	I	N	P	I	E	R	C	E	
L	A	L	O		I	D	O	L	S		T	A	R	T
I	M	A	T		O	L	L	I	E		E	L	I	A
K	A	N	E		N	E	A	T	S		R	E	N	T

PAGE 125

Binairo®

0	1	0	0	1	0	1	1	0	1	0	1
1	0	0	1	1	0	1	0	1	0	1	0
0	1	1	0	0	1	0	1	0	1	0	1
1	0	0	1	1	0	1	0	0	1	0	1
1	0	1	1	0	1	0	0	1	0	1	0
0	1	1	0	0	1	0	1	1	0	0	1
1	1	0	0	1	0	1	0	0	1	1	0
1	0	0	1	1	0	0	1	1	0	1	0
0	0	1	0	0	1	1	0	1	1	0	1
1	1	0	1	0	1	0	1	0	0	1	0
0	1	1	0	1	0	1	0	0	1	0	1
0	0	1	1	0	1	0	1	1	0	1	0

CHANGE ONE
BRAIN DRAIN

PAGE 126

Classic Sudoku

1	7	3	9	2	6	8	4	5
2	4	9	5	8	7	3	6	1
8	5	6	4	1	3	9	2	7
3	8	1	2	7	9	4	5	6
4	2	7	8	6	5	1	9	3
6	9	5	1	3	4	7	8	2
9	1	4	7	5	2	6	3	8
7	6	2	3	9	8	5	1	4
5	3	8	6	4	1	2	7	9

BLOCK ANAGRAM
Insulin

PAGE 127

Sport Maze

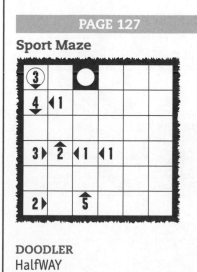

DOODLER
HalfWAY

PAGE 128

Oscar Winners

G	E	N	A		B	A	M	B	I			R	C	A
O	L	A	N		E	N	R	O	L		G	O	O	D
L	I	S	T		A	N	T	A	L		W	U	S	A
F	A	T	H	E	R	S			T	I	N	Y	T	I	M
			O	D	S			N	A	N				
B	E	R	N	I	E	S		T	O	H	E	L	E	N
O	X	E	Y	E		C	H	R	I	S	T	I	N	E
S	A	S	H		L	O	U	I	S			H	A	N	A
C	L	E	O	P	A	T	R	A		A	P	R	I	L
S	T	E	P	O	U	T		L	A	G	A	S	S	E
			K	E	R			G	E	L				
J	U	P	I	T	E	R		C	A	S	T	L	E	S
A	L	A	N		N	O	R	A	S		R	O	D	E
N	A	T	S		C	L	U	E	S		O	L	E	A
E	N	S			E	L	E	N	I		W	A	N	T

PAGE 129

Presidential Runners

B	A	C	H		R	A	M	S		O	C	A	L	A
L	I	L	A		O	L	A	N		N	A	D	A	L
O	D	E	R		B	A	R	A		E	M	A	I	L
G	E	O	R	G	E	M	C	G	O	V	E	R	N	
			I	N	R	O		B	O	O				
C	O	M	S	A	T		W	H	E	T		H	C	G
I	D	I	O	T		H	O	U	S	E	B	I	L	L
P	E	N	N		E	E	R	I	E		I	T	O	O
R	O	O	S	E	V	E	L	T		B	L	E	S	S
O	N	S		C	O	L	D		C	O	L	M	E	S
			U	K	R			D	O	O	M			
	M	I	C	H	A	E	L	D	U	K	A	K	I	S
T	E	S	L	A		L	E	A	R		H	Y	D	E
S	A	L	A	R		L	A	Y	S		E	L	L	A
P	L	A	N	T		E	L	S	E		R	E	E	L

PAGE 130

Binairo®

1	0	1	1	0	1	0	1	0	1	0
0	1	1	0	0	1	0	1	1	0	1
1	0	0	1	1	0	1	0	1	0	1
0	1	1	0	1	0	1	1	0	1	0
1	1	0	1	0	1	0	0	1	0	1
0	0	1	0	1	1	0	1	0	1	1
0	1	0	1	1	0	1	1	0	1	0
1	0	1	1	0	0	1	0	1	0	1
1	1	0	0	1	1	0	1	1	0	0
0	1	1	0	0	1	1	0	0	1	1
1	0	0	1	1	0	1	0	1	1	0

MAGIC SQUARE
There are 86 ways that the numbers can be added up to total 34. Apart from the 4 rows, 4 columns, and two diagonals, here are more which will help lead you to others. 9-14-3-8, 4-9-8-13, 15-8-9-2, 6-7-10-11, 15-14-3-2, 4-5-11-14

PAGE 131

Word Sudoku

B	P	S	D	R	I	V	E	A
I	E	V	A	S	P	B	D	R
R	A	D	B	E	V	S	I	P
P	D	E	S	B	A	I	R	V
V	I	R	E	P	D	A	S	B
A	S	B	V	I	R	D	P	E
D	B	P	R	A	S	E	V	I
E	V	I	P	D	B	R	A	S
S	R	A	I	V	E	P	B	D

DOODLER
SpONsor

PAGE 132

Sudoku X

1	7	5	8	6	3	2	4	9
4	2	9	7	5	1	3	8	6
8	3	6	4	9	2	5	7	1
5	6	1	9	3	4	7	2	8
3	9	8	2	7	5	6	1	4
7	4	2	6	1	8	9	3	5
6	5	3	1	8	7	4	9	2
9	1	4	3	2	6	8	5	7
2	8	7	5	4	9	1	6	3

SQUARE LINKS
SNOWDROP:
Snow, Nave, Oval, Well, Drop,
Rope, Open, Pens.

PAGE 133

Hizzoner

PAGE 134

Sport Maze

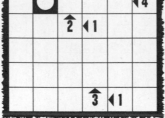

BLOCK ANAGRAM
RHABDOMANCER

PAGE 135

Mystery Letter

M. Together the blocks form a
series of letters from A to M.

THE SECURITY GUARD'S
PATROL

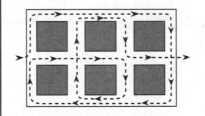

PAGE 136

Kakuro

MISSING LETTER PROVERB
Possession is nine points of
the law.

PAGE 137

Classic Sudoku

5	3	7	2	1	9	4	8	6
8	4	6	7	3	5	1	2	9
1	9	2	6	4	8	7	3	5
9	2	4	1	5	6	8	7	3
3	6	8	9	7	4	5	1	2
7	1	5	3	8	2	6	9	4
2	8	3	4	6	7	9	5	1
4	5	9	8	2	1	3	6	7
6	7	1	5	9	3	2	4	8

LETTER LINE
PLEASING
(Gap. Nil. Snipe.)

PAGE 138

Men of Letters

PAGE 139

State Mottos

PAGE 140

Sport Maze

A TIDY ORCHARD

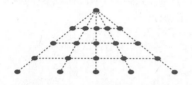

PAGE 141

Binairo®

I	I	O	O	I	O	I	O	I	O	O	I
O	O	I	O	I	I	O	I	O	I	O	I	O
I	I	O	I	O	O	I	I	O	O	I	O
O	O	I	O	I	O	I	O	I	I	O	I
I	I	O	I	O	I	O	O	I	O	I	O
I	O	I	O	I	O	I	O	I	O	I	O	O
O	O	I	O	I	O	I	I	O	O	I	I
O	I	O	I	O	I	O	O	I	I	O	I
I	O	O	I	I	O	I	O	O	I	I	O
O	O	I	O	O	I	O	I	O	I	I	O	I
O	I	O	I	O	O	I	I	O	I	O	O	I
I	I	O	I	I	O	O	I	O	I	O	O

SQUARE LINKS
S E E — S A W
E A R — A P E
E R R — W E E

PAGE 142

Word Sudoku

L	J	E	N	A	G	S	V	U
G	A	U	S	V	L	J	N	E
S	V	N	U	E	J	A	G	L
E	L	V	G	J	S	U	A	N
J	N	A	V	U	E	L	S	G
U	S	G	L	N	A	E	J	V
N	E	L	A	S	V	G	U	J
V	G	S	J	L	U	N	E	A
A	U	J	E	G	N	V	L	S

LETTER LINE
PRODUCED
(Our. Duped. Cup.)

PAGE 143

Themeless

PAGE 144

A+ Novels

PAGE 145

Binairo®

O	I	O	I	I	O	I	O	O	I	I
I	O	I	O	I	I	O	I	O	O	I
O	I	I	O	O	I	I	O	I	I	O
I	I	O	I	I	O	I	O	O	I	I	O	O
O	O	I	I	O	I	I	O	O	I	I
I	I	O	O	I	O	O	I	I	O	I
I	O	I	O	O	I	I	O	I	I	O
O	O	I	I	O	O	I	I	O	I	I
O	I	O	O	I	I	O	I	I	O	I
I	O	I	I	O	I	I	O	I	O	O
I	I	O	I	I	O	I	O	I	O	O

BLOCK ANAGRAM
ASTROLOGY

PAGE 146

Sudoku Twin

PAGE 147

Sport Maze

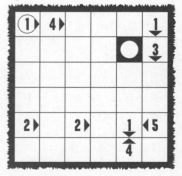

UNCANNY TURN
TWELVE PLUS ONE

PAGE 148

Classic Sudoku

4	3	7	6	2	5	9	8	1
9	5	1	3	7	8	2	6	4
6	8	2	4	1	9	5	7	3
2	1	9	5	8	4	7	3	6
3	7	4	9	6	2	8	1	5
8	6	5	1	3	7	4	9	2
5	4	6	8	9	1	3	2	7
7	9	3	2	5	6	1	4	8
1	2	8	7	4	3	6	5	9

DOODLER
RedEYES

PAGE 149

Kakuro

1	2	6		5	2		9	1
9	8		7	8	6		1	4
4	5	3	9		7	5		3
5		4				3	1	5
	8	1	2		1	6	3	
6	4		3	5	7		8	9
7	2	9		9	2	6		6
5		2		1		8	5	7
3	6	7	1		7	5	4	8

DELETE ONE
MINISTRY

PAGE 150

Parking Spaces

6565656. Starting in the upper left corner, per type of car there is always one car more and the cars alternate being parked nose inward and outward.

FIVES AND FOURS

S W O R D S P I T
T A B L E Z U L U
A B O V E S O A R
R A D A R M O O N

PAGE 151

Sudoku X

4	5	6	8	2	9	1	7	3
3	1	8	4	5	7	6	9	2
7	9	2	6	3	1	5	4	8
6	7	4	3	9	2	8	1	5
5	8	1	7	6	4	2	3	9
9	2	3	1	8	5	7	6	4
1	3	7	2	4	8	9	5	6
2	4	9	5	7	6	3	8	1
8	6	5	9	1	3	4	2	7

CHANGE ONE
GOOD MATCH

PAGE 152

Show Tunes

A	N	N	A		S	M	U	T	S		A	B	C	S
M	O	O	D		M	A	N	E	T		R	I	O	T
M	E	R	V		A	N	I	T	A		O	G	L	E
O	L	M	A	N	R	I	V	E	R		O	S	A	R
		N	O	T	A		T	A	M	P	
D	I	S	C	S		C	A	P	E	R		E	D	A
O	N	M	E		L	E	D	A		N	O	B	
G	L	A	S	S		M	A	N		L	I	D	D	Y
M	A	L		E	R	I	N		M	E	G	S	
A	W	L		L	E	A	S	H		S	I	R	E	S
		W	O	L	F		A	D	I	T	
E	R	O	S		I	L	O	V	E	P	A	R	I	S
M	A	R	A		N	O	L	A	N		T	O	R	O
M	I	L	K		E	V	E	N	T		O	M	A	R
A	D	D	A		D	E	G	A	S		R	E	N	T

PAGE 153

Pixel Fun

BRAINSNACK® © PETERFRANK ALL RIGHTS RESERVED

CHANGE THE NUMBER

    561
  + 254

    815

PAGE 154

Mr. Secretary

F	A	L	A		R	A	B	E		P	I	N	C	H
A	S	I	A		I	N	R	I		A	D	O	R	E
S	T	A	R		G	E	A	R		L	A	U	E	R
T	I	M	O	T	H	Y	G	E	I	T	H	N	E	R
		N	O	T	E	S		P	R	O	
S	A	M	B	A	S		B	O	O		S	H	A	
A	D	O	U	T		G	O	L	D	W	A	T	E	R
T	O	R	R		S	L	U	E	S		M	A	G	I
A	P	A	R	T	H	E	I	D		B	E	N	E	S
N	E	L		W	E	E		F	O	N	D	L	E	
		G	E	E		S	T	O	O	D	
L	A	W	R	E	N	C	E	S	U	M	M	E	R	S
U	B	O	A	T		A	G	A	R		E	L	I	A
L	A	N	C	E		R	U	N	T		N	E	L	L
U	T	T	E	R		L	E	A	H		T	A	L	E

PAGE 155

Binairo®

I	O	I	I	O	I	I	O	O	I	O	O
I	I	O	O	I	I	O	I	O	I	O	O
O	I	O	I	O	O	I	O	I	O	I	I
O	O	I	I	O	I	O	I	I	O	I	O
I	I	O	O	I	O	I	I	O	I	O	O
I	O	I	I	O	I	O	O	I	I	O	I
O	I	I	O	I	O	I	O	I	O	I	O
I	O	O	I	I	O	O	I	O	I	O	I
O	O	I	O	O	I	I	O	I	O	I	I
O	I	O	I	O	I	O	I	O	I	I	O
I	O	I	O	I	O	I	O	O	I	O	I
O	I	O	O	I	O	O	I	I	O	I	I

CHANGELINGS

WASHINGTON
COPENHAGEN
ALEXANDRIA

PAGE 156

Themeless

A	N	I	S	T	O	N		O	C	T	O	P	U	S
L	A	V	E	R	N	E		C	A	R	R	E	R	E
P	R	O	M	I	S	E		T	R	E	A	T	E	D
S	C	R	I	B	E		E	S	T	E	
		N	U	T	S		A	L	T	E	R	E	D
A	S	C	O	T		I	M	P	E	L		B	T	U
T	O	O	L	E		L	A	P	S	E		O	A	R
R	U	N	E		C	E	D	E	S		T	Y	P	E
A	T	T		C	O	N	G	A		S	E	L	E	S
M	E	R		U	L	C	E	R		T	R	E	S	S
P	R	A	T	T	L	E		S	E	E	R	
		C	I	R	E		A	R	A	R	A	T
C	O	T	T	A	G	E		T	R	I	P	O	L	I
C	R	E	A	T	E	S		A	L	L	I	S	O	N
S	A	D	N	E	S	S		T	E	E	N	A	G	E

PAGE 157

Pixel Fun

BLOCK ANAGRAM
CLAIRVOYANT

PAGE 158

Lord Stanley's Cup

T	R	I	G		T	R	E	E	S		A	L	F	S
R	E	N	O		U	I	N	T	A		R	I	L	E
A	F	A	R		L	A	T	E	R		I	G	E	T
P	E	N	G	U	I	N	S		A	L	O	H	A	S
P	R	E	E	M	P	T		A	N	E	S	T	
			O	P	S		R	E	D	W	I	N	G	S
P	R	I	U	S		R	E	S	O	D		I	O	U
L	E	S	S		E	A	S	O	N		S	N	O	B
U	A	L		A	D	R	I	P		S	I	G	N	S
S	P	A	C	E	M	E	N		E	N	D			
		N	E	R	O	S		P	R	I	E	S	T	S
H	U	D	S	O	N		M	O	N	T	R	E	A	L
O	R	E	S		T	H	A	N	E		E	L	L	A
W	A	R	N		O	B	I	T	S		A	M	E	N
E	L	S	A		N	O	N	E	T		L	A	S	T

PAGE 159

Binairo®

O	I	O	I	I	O	I	O	I	O	I
O	O	I	I	O	I	I	O	I	O	I
I	O	I	O	I	I	O	I	O	I	O
I	I	O	I	I	O	O	I	O	O	I
O	I	I	O	O	I	I	O	I	I	O
I	O	I	O	I	O	I	I	O	I	O
I	O	O	I	O	I	O	I	I	O	I
O	I	I	O	O	I	I	O	O	I	I
I	I	O	I	I	O	O	I	I	O	O
O	O	I	I	O	O	I	I	O	I	I
I	I	O	O	I	I	O	O	I	I	O

BLOCK ANAGRAM
TELEPATHY

PAGE 160

The President's Men

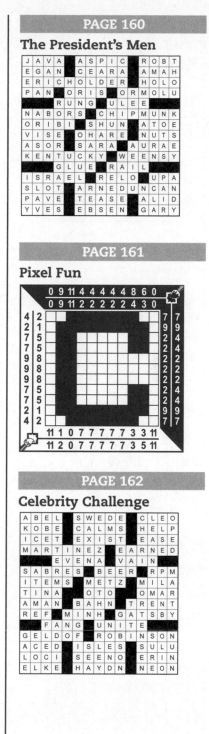

PAGE 161

Pixel Fun

PAGE 162

Celebrity Challenge

PAGE 163

Binairo®

I	I	O	O	I	O	I	O	I	I	O	O
I	I	O	I	O	O	I	O	I	O	I	O
O	O	I	I	O	I	O	I	O	I	O	I
I	I	O	O	I	O	O	I	I	O	O	I
O	O	I	I	O	I	I	O	O	I	I	O
O	I	I	O	O	I	O	I	O	O	I	I
I	O	O	I	I	O	O	I	I	O	O	I
O	I	I	O	I	O	I	O	O	I	I	O
I	O	O	I	O	I	O	I	O	I	O	I
O	I	I	O	I	I	O	O	I	O	I	O
I	I	O	I	I	O	I	I	O	I	O	O
O	O	I	O	O	I	I	O	I	O	I	I

DOODLER
THunderCloud

PAGE 164

Classic Co-stars

PAGE 165

Pixel Fun

CROSS WORD?
Temperament

PAGE 166
Oil on Canvas

T	S	A	R	S		R	O	A	N		H	Y	D	E
A	L	L	O	T		A	L	S	O		E	V	E	R
L	E	O	N	E		V	E	I	N		R	E	N	T
E	D	G	A	R	D	E	G	A	S		E	S	S	E
			I	O	N			E	A	S	T			
C	A	J	O	L	E		T	A	N	G		A	N	G
E	R	A	S	E		M	A	N	S	E		N	O	R
D	E	M	O		M	A	I	N	E		O	G	L	E
E	N	E		M	A	R	L	A		A	C	U	T	E
D	A	S		A	R	C	S		P	L	A	Y	E	R
	E	D	D	Y			I	R	A					
U	L	N	A		J	A	N	V	E	R	M	E	E	R
P	O	S	T		A	R	E	A		M	O	R	S	E
O	B	O	E		N	O	O	N		E	N	A	T	E
N	O	R	D		E	N	N	A		D	O	T	E	D

PAGE 167
Binairo®

I	I	O	I	O	I	O	I	O	I	O
I	I	O	I	O	I	I	O	I	O	O
O	O	I	O	I	O	I	I	O	I	I
I	O	O	I	O	I	O	I	I	O	I
O	I	I	O	I	O	I	O	I	I	O
I	I	O	O	I	O	I	O	I	I	O
I	O	I	I	O	I	O	O	I	O	I
O	O	I	O	I	I	O	I	I	O	I
I	I	O	I	I	O	I	O	O	I	O
O	O	I	I	O	O	I	I	O	I	I
O	I	I	O	I	I	O	O	I	O	I

BLOCK ANAGRAM
TAROT CARD

PAGE 168
Set in New York

H	E	L	P		S	P	O	T	S		D	O	O	R
A	L	A	R		T	O	N	I	O		O	G	R	E
R	A	V	I		A	C	T	E	D		G	L	A	D
P	L	A	N		R	U	H	R		A	D	E	L	A
		C	U	R	S	E		D	E	A	D	E	N	
L	O	V	E	L	Y		W	O	R	R	Y			
I	D	I	O	M		J	A	N	E		A	C	R	E
F	I	E	F		H	A	T	E	D		F	L	A	P
T	E	S	T		I	V	E	S		S	T	A	G	E
	H	A	G	A	R		P	E	E	W	E	E		
J	O	S	E	P	H		F	L	A	I	R			
E	D	I	C	T		C	R	A	T		N	I	N	A
S	I	S	I		S	H	O	R	T		O	D	O	R
S	L	A	T		R	A	N	G	O		O	L	I	N
E	E	L	Y		A	N	T	O	N		N	E	R	O

PAGE 169
Pixel Fun

CHUCKLER
Giggling

PAGE 170
Winning Spelling Bee Words

L	O	A	D		D	E	N	E	B		N	C	O	S
A	C	L	U		E	D	E	M	A		A	A	R	P
P	E	E	L		A	D	L	I	B		S	T	A	R
S	A	U	C	I	L	Y		T	U	S	C	A	N	Y
E	N	T	I	R	E			S	L	A	M			
		M	A	R	S		T	H	E	R	A	P	Y	
E	M	C	E	E		C	O	R	K	Y		R	A	E
P	A	R	R		I	O	N	I	A		V	A	C	A
I	W	O		E	N	R	O	L		O	I	N	K	S
C	R	I	S	P	I	N		L	U	N	G			
	S	U	E	T			P	I	N	A	T	A		
E	P	S	T	E	I	N		A	L	T	E	R	E	R
A	L	A	R		A	C	C	R	A		T	I	R	E
T	U	N	A		L	A	P	I	N		T	E	R	N
S	G	T	S		S	A	L	A	D		E	L	A	T

PAGE 171
Binairo®

O	O	I	I	O	I	O	I	O	I	I
I	I	O	I	I	O	I	O	O	I	O
O	I	I	O	I	I	O	I	I	O	O
I	O	I	I	O	I	O	I	O	O	I
O	I	O	I	I	O	I	O	I	I	O
I	I	O	O	I	O	I	O	O	I	I
O	O	I	I	O	I	O	I	I	O	I
I	I	O	O	I	O	I	O	I	I	O
O	O	I	O	I	O	I	I	O	I	I
I	I	O	I	O	I	O	I	I	O	O
I	O	I	O	O	I	I	O	I	O	I

UNCANNY TURN
DIRTY ROOM

PAGE 172
Dancing with Fred

O	W	L			A	L	F	R	E			P	O	T
V	I	E	D		E	E	L	E	D		S	A	N	E
A	N	N	A		N	O	Y	E	S		I	R	E	D
L	E	A	D		E	N	I	D		P	L	E	A	D
			D	R	A	I	N		L	I	K	E	L	Y
T	R	O	Y	E	S		G	R	I	N	S			
H	O	L	L	Y		A	D	A	M		T	I	E	D
I	D	E	O		C	R	O	C	E		O	D	I	E
N	E	O	N		H	O	W	E		A	C	O	R	N
			G	L	E	N	N		O	A	K	L	E	Y
M	A	I	L	E	R		T	E	R	R	I			
E	R	R	E	D		M	O	A	N		N	U	N	S
C	L	O	G		H	A	R	T	E		G	N	A	T
C	O	N	S		O	S	I	E	R		S	I	L	O
A	S	S			P	H	O	N	Y			T	A	P

PAGE 173
Binairo®

I	O	I	I	O	I	O	O	I	I	O
O	I	I	O	O	I	O	I	O	I	I
I	O	O	I	I	O	I	O	I	O	I
O	I	I	O	I	O	I	O	I	I	O
O	I	O	I	O	I	O	I	O	I	I
I	O	I	O	I	O	I	O	I	O	I
I	I	O	O	I	I	O	I	O	I	O
O	O	I	I	O	I	I	O	I	O	I
O	I	O	I	I	O	I	I	O	I	O
I	O	I	O	O	I	O	I	I	O	I
I	I	O	I	I	O	I	O	I	O	O

FIRST THINGS FIRST
We will never forget you.

PAGE 174
Eclectic Mix

V	E	R	B		J	I	L	L	S		S	A	F	E
E	P	E	E		A	D	I	E	U		O	R	A	L
T	I	D	E		M	E	E	T	S		M	I	N	K
S	C	O	T	S	M	A	N		P	L	E	A	S	E
			H	E	E	L		S	E	E	R			
A	C	C	O	R	D		S	I	N	I	S	T	E	R
S	O	A	V	E		V	A	T	S		E	A	V	E
P	A	N	E		S	A	D	I	E		T	R	E	E
I	C	O	N		E	G	A	N		A	M	E	N	D
C	H	E	S	T	N	U	T		B	R	A	S	S	Y
			S	I	T	E		M	E	N	U			
A	D	V	I	S	E		M	A	H	O	G	A	N	Y
H	O	A	X		N	A	O	M	I		H	O	Y	A
E	R	S	T		C	H	A	I	N		A	N	E	W
M	Y	T	H		E	A	S	E	D		M	E	T	S